Career Guide and Directory for Immigrant Professionals

Lesley Kamenshine

Solveig Fisher, Maureen Ickrath, Ruth Kaplan,
and Keke Lowe, Contributors

The Scarecrow Press, Inc.
Lanham, Maryland, and Oxford
2003

SCARECROW PRESS, INC.

Published in the United States of America by Scarecrow Press, Inc.
A wholly owned subsidiary of
The Rowman & Littlefield Publishing Group, Inc.
4501 Forbes Boulevard, Suite 200, Lanham, Maryland 20706
www.scarecrowpress.com

PO Box 317
Oxford
OX2 9RU, UK

British Library Cataloguing in Publication Information Available

Library of Congress Cataloging-in-Publication Data

Kamenshine, Lesley.
  Career guide and directory for immigrant professionals / Lesley Kamenshine ;
Solveig Fisher . . . [et al.], contributors.
    p. cm.
Includes bibliographical references and index.
  ISBN 0-8108-4842-2 (pbk. : alk. paper)
  1. Vocational guidance—United States—Handbooks, manuals, etc.
  2. Vocational guidance for minorities—Handbooks, manuals, etc.
  3. Immigrants—Employment—Handbooks, manuals, etc. I. Title.
HF5382.5.U5 K288 2003
331.7'02'08691—dc21   2003010900

∞™ The paper used in this publication meets the minimum requirements of
American National Standard for Information Sciences—Permanence of Paper
for Printed Library Materials, ANSI/NISO Z39.48-1992

Manufactured in the United States of America.

Contents

Acknowledgments   v

Introduction   vii

How to Use This Directory   ix

1   Improving Your American English   1
    Quick Reference   12
    • ESL Course Names
    • Test Types
    Resource Directory   13
    • Universities and Four-Year Colleges That Offer ESL Programs
    • Community College Programs
    • Private/Corporate Language Programs
    • Adult Education Programs
    • Professional Test Preparation Center

2   Discovering Your Career Options   33
    Quick Reference   43
    • Alternative Career Examples
    • Certification and Licensure Definitions
    • Independent Contractor and Employee Definition
    • Licensing Steps
    • World of Associations in the U.S.
    Resource Directory   56
    • Career Guidance
    • Licensing Contact Examples
    • Licensing Contacts for Accounting Professionals

- Licensing Contacts for Engineering Professionals
- Licensing Contacts for Health Professionals
- Licensing Contacts for Attorneys
- Entrepreneurial Help

3 Making American Higher Education Work for You   99
Quick Reference   108
- Educational Institutions of Higher Learning
- An Educational Institution's Credentials
- When Schools Come to You
Resource Directory   116
- Higher Education Institutions

4 Exploring Financial Assistance for Your Education   139
Quick Reference   147
- Federal Financial Aid Opportunities
- General Eligibility Criteria and Restrictions for Federal
  Educational Financial Aid
- Tips for Completing FAFSA

Appendixes
A: Useful Phone Numbers, Agencies, and General Resources   153
B: Pre-Resume Questionnaire   159
C: Getting Your Foreign Credentials Evaluated   165
D: Academic Programs in the United States—
  and How to Find Schools That Offer Them   169

Index   198

About the Author and Contributors   203

Acknowledgments

This directory has not been a one-person endeavor. Thanks so much to the many people who have made it possible. Solveig Fisher, Maureen Ickrath, Ruth Kaplan, and Keke Lowe combined their individual expertise with mine for a unique synergism that could guide new Americans with their career plans.

Thanks to officials at federal and state education agencies, professional associations, as well as county libraries, for generously sharing their knowledge and help. Heartfelt thanks to Carol Buchanan, Suzanne Carbone, Cindy Counihan, Alan Edwards, Julia Funaki, Pam Hagan, Lois Haglund, Lynn Hough, Michael Kiphart, Roslyn Korb, Keondra Nicholas, Rick Patterson, Marilyn Thornton, and Pete White, among others.

Every effort has been made to check the accuracy of the resource directories with the dedication of librarians Wanda Anastasi, Mae Daughtery, Jennifer Miller, and Gwen O'Brien. Benita Fox was ever ready—and cheerful—to do word processing. Thanks also to Toa Do of the Business Development Assistance Group in Fairfax, who made his staff available to help with fact checking, if that became necessary.

Most significantly, I appreciate the steady hand of Kim Tabor, my editor at Scarecrow Press, and thank her for her enthusiasm and integrity—you can sense early on when you have a terrific editor. Kudos to Kellie Hagan, production editor, who worked intensively and creatively with a complicated layout and a tight deadline. And thanks to Solveig Fisher for applying her editorial skills at several critical stages.

My family encouraged me with my dream every day of the years it has taken to bring out this directory. Without their love and unending patience, this directory would not have developed. "Thanks" will never be enough.

Introduction

Developing this directory has been a labor of love. The concept of helping immigrant professionals to find their niche as part of the American Dream has been in our consciousness for several years. It has been painful to see doctors, engineers, and other educated immigrants work in positions far below their potential. We thought perhaps they just didn't know enough about the American system to make it work for them.

In 1999, I invited several acquaintances—all of us are either immigrants or the children of immigrants—to join me in sharing our knowledge with new Americans. Our enthusiasm has been unwavering. Along the way, our small group became good friends!

Special thanks to Nancy-Pat Weaver, who gave the project her work on chapter 4, when she withdrew because of her busy schedule. I also want to thank Helena Myers-Wright, a member of our original group who moved to Germany before this project was completed.

I hope this directory will help guide you to the American Dream. Welcome!

How to Use This Directory

GENERAL INFORMATION

This directory provides you with general information about the American culture and processes for improving your American English, developing your understanding of careers and American higher education, and applying for educational financial aid. In addition to federal government resources, where applicable, state, local resources, and private resources are provided for the District of Columbia, Maryland suburbs, and northern Virginia.

WASHINGTON METROPOLITAN AREA

The U.S. Census 2000 (www.census.gov/population/estimates/metro-city/99mfips.txt) defines the Washington, D.C., primary metropolitan statistical area as follows:

- District of Columbia
- The following counties in Maryland: Calvert, Charles, Frederick, Montgomery, and Prince George's
- The following counties in Virginia: Arlington, Clarke, Culpeper, Fairfax, Fauquier, King George, Loudoun, Prince William, Spotsylvania, Stafford, and Warren
- The following cities in Virginia: Alexandria, Fairfax, Falls Church, Fredericksburg, Manassas, and Manassas Park
- The following counties in West Virginia: Berkeley and Jefferson counties

The guide/directory covers the District of Columbia, Maryland, and Northern Virginia. In Northern Virginia, we focus on areas with the largest immigrant populations: the counties of Fairfax, Prince William, and Loudoun; and the cities of Fairfax, Arlington, Alexandria, and Manassas. In addition some institutions have been included from Howard County, Maryland.

CHAPTERS

Each chapter introduces you to how the American system works so you can save time and get started with your exploration. "First steps" checklists appear in each chapter, suggesting immediate actions for you.

Quick Reference. In a few paragraphs or pages, we highlight and explain basic concepts or provide tips to help you better use the American system.

Resource Directory. We provide you with multiple resources to improve your English, examine your career, and further your education. Chapter 4, "Exploring Financial Assistance for Your Education," relies on websites offered throughout the chapter rather than a resource directory. Keep in mind that we provide you with representative listings, which are not meant to be comprehensive. We do not endorse any listing. We strongly encourage you to check out listings and make personal visits before you make any decisions. Annotations that accompany certain listings represent information provided by the institution either in its materials or through a conversation with its representatives; annotations do not represent an evaluation or endorsement of the institution or agency.

YOUR PRIORITIES

The chapters in this guide do not need to be read in a particular order. Instead, we recommend that you start with what is most crucial to you.

- If your American English (pronunciation, grammar, and speaking and listening skills) needs a serious boost for you to communicate effectively in the workplace, start with chapter 1, "Improving Your American English."
- If your career is most crucial, begin with chapter 2, "Discovering Your Career Options."

- If you need to attend school, start with chapter 3, "Making American Higher Education Work for You."
- If money is important, begin with chapter 4, "Exploring Financial Assistance for Your Education."

USEFUL PHONE NUMBERS
AND CONTACT INFORMATION

Phone Numbers. No long distance numbers are identified, since long distance calling depends on your location and phone service relative to the number you are dialing in the Washington region. However, the following phone numbers are toll-free and do require you to dial 1 before the number: 800, 866, 877, and 888.

E-mail Addresses. This directory provides many e-mail addresses. As you know, these can change without notice. Therefore, with a few exceptions, we provide institutional rather than individual e-mail addresses. If it's not listed in the resource directory, check the website for an e-mail link or call the institution and request the e-mail address.

Websites. Websites are listed without the introductory *http://*, with a few exceptions. In many cases, *www.* has also been removed. All sites were tested as of April 2003. If the site does not work, here are some suggestions:

- Check that you wrote the site correctly in your notes.
- Check that you have entered the address correctly on the web.
- Add or delete *http://* before *www.*
- Add or delete *www.* whether or not *http://* exists.
- Eliminate the extended address to the first forward slash in the address, after the main page web listing; this move will allow you to access the site's home page. Once at the home page, you can usually left click your mouse to another page within the website or to links with another website.

Note: Where information seemed difficult to find, we include links to subsequent pages in our effort to bring you closer to the information you need (identified below the website as *clicks*). We are aware that these links sometimes change as web pages are updated, so you may find new sites rather than those we have identified.

Chapter One

Improving Your American English

Improving your American English is *very* important for an immigrant professional. When you speak and write well, you also project confidence and competence in your profession. A good vocabulary, standard grammar, and clear pronunciation are all necessary for everyday life and the workplace.

In addition, for many professional jobs, an immigrant must write very well, speak fluently, and understand rapid, spoken, idiomatic American English. Even professionals from other English-speaking countries may have some language problems, especially with pronunciation, vocabulary, or idioms. There are many varieties of the English language, and each version—British English, Indian English, African English, Jamaican English, or any other English—will have some differences from American English. In the United States, however, American English is expected in the workplace.

WAYS TO LEARN AMERICAN ENGLISH

There are many ways to practice your English language skills:

- Watch TV (with captions, if available)
- Watch public television broadcasts of ESL (English as a Second Language) programs
- Listen to the radio (try news programs that are repeated, such as on WTOP)

1

- Listen to English language tapes or CDs (while driving, exercising, relaxing)
- Watch English movies (particularly with subtitles in your language)
- Speak to English speakers (neighbors, store clerks, coworkers, and others)
- Read American books, magazines, newspapers
- Work at an entry-level job, a volunteer job, or an apprenticeship
- Use Internet ESL resources (see "Other Language Resources," page 9)
- Attend English as a Second Language courses (called ESL or ESOL; see "ESL Course Names," page 12)

ENGLISH COURSES AND SCHOOLS

There are many English-language programs in the Washington metropolitan region. Courses are available for almost all language levels, time schedules, and budgets.

General Information

Intensity. The types of courses are frequently referred to as intensive, semi-intensive, and nonintensive. Intensive courses meet several times a week, often for four or five days, for several hours a day ("full-time"). Semi-intensive courses are held two or more days a week, but with fewer total hours than intensive ones. Nonintensive courses may meet once or twice a week, and the time spent in the classroom is shorter.

Course Names. Course names may be confusing. You will find English classes and programs with a variety of different titles and abbreviations (see "Quick Reference, ESL Course Names," later in this chapter). Do not be too concerned about the name of your course; pay more attention to the level, quality, and intensity of the instruction.

Courses are most commonly referred to as ESL, which stands for English as a Second Language, or ESOL, which stands for English for/to Speakers of Other Languages. In the Washington area, most English programs in elementary and secondary schools are called ESOL, while courses offered by colleges are often called ESL. Educators across the country do not agree on which term is best to use. One of their objections to English as a *Second* Language is that many students in the

United States are studying English as their third or fourth language, not their second one!

Placement Tests. Students usually take a placement or assessment test before they are placed in a particular program or class. There are several standardized tests used by colleges and other schools, and the schools will tell you which one they require.

The best-known test is the TOEFL, Test of English as a Foreign Language. Given around the world, this examination tests listening comprehension, structure, reading comprehension, and writing. Students abroad often take this exam before applying to a U.S. college or university. If a student receives a sufficiently high score on the TOEFL, the student may be accepted directly into a degree program at a U.S. college or university. On the basis of their TOEFL scores, many students are told that they have to take some ESL courses before they can enter a regular college degree program. It is possible to take the TOEFL several times to improve your score and be accepted into the college program of your choice. TOEFL tests are given by a private company; certain schools administer Institutional TOEFL exams, but only to their own students. Changes are being made in the format of the TOEFL, and a speaking test (TAST) will be added by 2005. For information about locations and dates, the website is www.toefl.org/.

In the Washington region, many schools do not require the TOEFL. However, they will ask prospective students to take the Michigan, CELT, or another placement test. The schools themselves usually administer these tests. Normally, a student applies to a school and then is given an appointment to take the test that the school requires. For a list of placement tests, along with their abbreviations and explanations, see "Quick Reference, Test Types," later in this chapter.

What's Best for You?

An immigrant professional should look for the school or program that prepares him best for his personal career goals. There are several factors to consider:

Level. What level of English do you need to study first?

Time. How fast do you need to learn English? How many hours a week can you spend in class and on homework and practice?

Money. How much money can you afford to pay for English classes?

Location. What programs can you attend by using public transportation or by driving?

Schedule. When do you need to begin your classes?

Tip: Universities, four-year colleges, community colleges, and adult education programs usually follow a set academic calendar. If you want to begin your English studies after the beginning of an academic semester, consider calling some private language schools. Many of them begin classes between academic semesters, or even when a number of students request a certain course.

No matter what level of English you study, be aware that *language learning takes time, exposure, and lots and lots of practice.* Use every possible opportunity to practice your English-language skills outside of the classroom, and surround yourself with as much spoken and written English as you can.

The following are *general* guidelines and suggestions for finding an English program for you. The suggestions take into account a student's language level in addition to time and financial constraints. Not every type of school listed will have the program you are looking for, but many will. Characteristics of the different programs suggested here are described in detail in the section "Characteristics of Language Programs" (later in this chapter).

Beginning American English Students. Do you need to learn fast? Look for intensive programs. Check private language schools, English-language institutes, community colleges, or four-year colleges and universities. Do you have little time or money? Look for semi-intensive or nonintensive programs. Check adult education courses (some are free), private language schools, or continuing education departments of community colleges.

Intermediate American English Students. Do you need to learn fast? Look for intensive courses at English-language institutes, private language schools, four-year colleges and universities, or community colleges. Do you have little time or money? Perhaps you have a job or family responsibilities. Look for semi-intensive or nonintensive courses at community colleges, private language schools, four-year colleges and universities, or English-language institutes.

Advanced American English Students. Look for advanced courses at four-year colleges and universities, community colleges, English-language institutes, or private language schools. Advanced students may not need an intensive course. However, they might benefit from internships or special programs that help participants gain the technical vocabulary and speaking style used in a profession. Ask if such programs exist in your field at colleges, universities, and professional organizations.

Sometimes an advanced student may prefer to take a course to refresh his or her English skills but does not want the stress of taking tests or receiving a grade. In such a case, the student should inquire if it is possible to "audit" a course. Auditing means taking a class but not receiving a grade or college credit. Be aware that if your employer is paying for a course, he may require you to take it for credit and present a passing grade.

Questions to Ask before Enrolling in an English Program

Try to get as much information as possible before you enroll in and pay for an English course. Here are some questions to consider asking:

- Is a placement test given to place students at the proper levels?
- What are the background and training of the teachers? (Teachers trained in TESOL, linguistics, or a foreign language may be more effective when teaching grammar and pronunciation.)
- What skills are emphasized in the courses? Speaking? Listening? Reading? Writing? Grammar? Vocabulary? Pronunciation?
- Are the courses designed for educated adults? What percentage of the students in the class has had some higher education in another country? What percentage of the students has already finished professional training in another country?
- Are the students in the program immigrants who intend to stay in the United States or students who came to the United States to study English and intend to return to their home countries? (This may affect the focus or intensity of the course.)
- How large are the classes? (Classes may range from as few as three to over thirty-five students.)
- How many hours of instruction are offered in each course? (Consider your personal learning style, the cost, and the speed at which you need to learn English.)
- How long is each lesson?
- When are the courses offered? Daytime? Evenings? Weekends?
- Where are the courses held? Can you get there by public transportation or car?

- How much do the courses cost?
- Is financial aid available? Is it given by the school, the government, or your employer?
- Is there a language lab for practice after course hours?
- Do the courses help to satisfy a language requirement for a particular career program or for occupational licensing?
- Are there English courses for professionals in a particular field? Do courses emphasize the technical vocabulary of that field? (School websites may be a good place to begin your search.)

Characteristics of Language Programs

Different types of schools emphasize different language skills and styles of American English. For example, some programs emphasize "academic" English, which prepares students for college-level work. Other courses contain more practice in speaking, stressing pronunciation, fluency, and practical, everyday English. Courses in adult education programs often emphasize these skills. Still other courses integrate oral and written language skills. The following list gives the main emphasis and other details of the ESL programs at different institutions and schools.

Four-Year Colleges and Universities

- Usually teach academic English courses to prepare students to take college-level courses and to earn degrees at U.S. colleges and universities.
- Students must take an English placement exam or present a TOEFL score.
- Emphasis is on writing, reading, advanced vocabulary.
- Speaking/listening classes emphasize formal spoken English, academic language, note taking.
- Courses usually follow the academic calendar and are a semester in length.
- Some have *English-language institutes,* which offer intensive courses to students from abroad who hold student visas as well as to other non-native students. (When students finish their studies at English-language institutes, they may apply to the college or university they are attending or to other colleges and universities in the United States.)

- Some have specialized courses for specific professions, e.g., Business English.
- May be more expensive than other programs.

Community Colleges, Academic Programs

- Require a placement test that students must pass at a certain level (often low-intermediate or intermediate).
- Follow a set sequence of courses that must be passed to advance to regular college courses.
- Emphasize writing, grammar, vocabulary, reading; some courses develop speaking, listening, and note-taking skills.
- Courses follow the academic calendar and are usually a semester in length.
- Courses may be less expensive than those at four-year colleges and universities.

Community Colleges, Continuing Education Courses

- Provide pre-academic training for students who want to enter the academic program but lack the necessary English skills.
- Provide general English courses at several levels for students who want to speak, read, and write better but are not working toward a degree.
- May provide courses for individual language skills, such as conversation or reading or vocabulary development.
- May provide specialized courses for more advanced students, such as English for professionals or business English.
- Courses may begin throughout the year, not just at the beginning of a semester.
- Courses vary in length and intensity.
- Grades may or may not be given.
- Courses may be less expensive than those at four-year colleges and universities.

Private/Corporate Language Schools

- Offer English classes for a variety of purposes and levels.
- Many give beginning English courses for new arrivals.
- Some give advanced courses for businesspeople, diplomats, and others.

- Costs vary from very reasonable to very expensive.
- Some offer intensive courses; some offer part-time courses.
- Courses may begin throughout the year.
- Classes may be small.
- Some may tailor courses to the needs of an individual student or a group of students.
- Some offer very specialized courses for select groups (e.g., diplomats).
- Some specialize in students from abroad who intend to return to their countries; these schools may assist students with student visas and finding housing or lodging with an American family.

Adult Education Courses Offered by Public School Systems

- Usually offer beginning-level classes.
- May emphasize "survival" English skills to help students become more comfortable in their communities and find jobs.
- Many are inexpensive or free.
- Some offer intermediate-level classes; a few give advanced classes.
- Often very popular; classes may be crowded (arrive early to register).
- Usually give a simple placement test, either written or spoken.
- Classes usually meet twice a week on weekdays, often in the evening, or on Saturdays.

Other Community-Based Adult Education Programs

- Classes may be sponsored by religious, ethnic, or civic groups (often beginning level).
- Conversation groups (for practicing speaking) may be sponsored by libraries and other civic groups.
- Instructors may or may not be trained in language teaching.
- Literacy groups provide volunteer tutors to teach reading and writing one-on-one (free, but there is often a long waiting list).
- Most programs are very inexpensive or free.
- Programs are nonintensive, usually meeting once or twice a week.

Test Preparation Schools

- Prepare nonnative students for important tests, such as TOEFL (Test of English as a Foreign Language) and USMLE (United States Medical Licensing Examination). Students must pass an English exam before taking the USMLE.

OTHER LANGUAGE RESOURCES

Websites

There are numerous websites that offer English lessons and help for students of English as a second language. Some may be very useful for beginning students who are learning English, others may offer needed practice and review for intermediate students, while still others may help advanced students who have specific questions. Here are some things to consider when looking for a website to practice your English:

- Is the English on the website American English (from the United States or Canada)? Many good websites offer international or British English, but be aware that there are some vocabulary and spelling differences between American and British English.
- Is the website free, or is there a charge for the program?
- Does the website offer a complete English course, or does it offer exercises, information, answers to questions, or the opportunity to chat online with other English learners or teachers?
- Is the website primarily for students or for teachers?
- Is there an audio component? Do you have the computer equipment necessary to listen?
- When was the website last updated, or how often is the website updated?

New websites may appear and old ones may change. The following are a few good Internet sources for students who want information about ESL and who want to study English online:

Dave's ESL Café. (www.eslcafe.com and www.eslcafe.com/search/Online_English_Courses) One of the most popular and useful online resources for students; frequently updated; includes an ESL Web Guide to Online English Courses.

The ESL Quiz Center. (www.pacificnet.net/~sperling/quiz/) Quizzes, which can also be accessed from Dave's ESL Café.

English as a Second Language. (www.rong-chang.com) Information on using websites to learn English; frequently updated; good links for business English and English for specific purposes (ESP).

ESL Gold. (www.eslgold.com/) Materials free to ESL students and teachers; includes phrases for conversation, with audio, picture dictionary, academic vocabulary exercises, and links to ESL materials on the Internet.

Purdue University Online Writing Lab. (owl.english.purdue.edu) Click Handouts and Materials, then English as a Second Language (ESL) Resources, Handouts, and Exercises. Helpful materials from a large U.S. university writing center.

WATESOL's ESL Resources. (www.watesol.org) Click ESL Resources. A lengthy list of websites and other resources compiled by the Washington Area Teachers of English for Speakers of Other Languages.

The following sites have audio components (streaming or downloadable to a disk) for practicing listening and speaking:

American English Pronunciation. (eleaston.com/pronunciation/) Includes explanations of consonant and vowel formation, reductions, grammatical ending pronunciations, and other subtle differences.

Pronunciation Links. (eleaston.com/pronunciation/links.html) Gives links to other sites offering pronunciation practice, activities, and information.

Learning English Online. (www.aec.ukans.edu/leo/index.html) From the Applied English Center at the University of Kansas; has a good list of featured sites.

Randall's ESL Cyber Listening Lab. (www.esl-lab.com) For self-directed study; includes listening quizzes for different levels, long conversations, and short listening exercises.

The websites listed above appeared in the Harnessing Technology web page, www.alri.org/harness.html, and The Literacy List, www.alri.org/litlist/esolwebsites.html. You can also find useful websites by typing in English as a Second Language or a related subject in a computer's search engine.

General ESL Books, Tapes, and CDs

There are hundreds of books written to teach English as a second language for all levels of language learning. They cover all the components of language: grammar, reading, writing, vocabulary, idioms, speaking, listening, and pronunciation. Before buying any new book, ask an English teacher if he or she recommends the book for your level and purposes. If you intend to take an ESL class, buy the book that the instructor recommends. If you want more information and advice about a particular book, you might go online and ask your questions there. Teachers and students can offer you helpful advice.

There are also many tapes and CDs that help you with language skills. Libraries are a good first place to look for recordings. It doesn't cost anything to listen to a recording. If you find a tape or CD that is helpful, you may want to buy it for more practice. Be aware that in stores, most tapes and CDs are wrapped in plastic and cannot be returned once they are opened.

Books for Technical/Professional Language and Vocabulary

You might look for books that explain and develop the technical vocabulary and communication style of your profession. The following are some examples. Before you buy a particular book, ask a teacher or another professional if the language in the book is appropriate for your needs.

Campbell, Elaine. *ESL Resource Book for Engineers and Scientists.* New York: John Wiley & Sons, 1995.
The Houghton Mifflin Brief Accounting Dictionary. Boston: Houghton Mifflin, 2000.
Lee, Debra S., J.D., Charles Hall, and Marsha Hurley, J.D. *American Legal English: Using Language in Legal Contexts.* Ann Arbor, Mich.: The University of Michigan Press, 1999.
Mascull, Bill. *Business Vocabulary in Use.* New York: Cambridge University Press, 2002.
Maher, John Christopher. *International Medical Communication in English.* Ann Arbor, Mich.: The University of Michigan Press, 1992.
Shulman, Myra. *Selected Readings in Business, Millennium Edition.* Ann Arbor, Mich.: The University of Michigan Press, 2003.

Private Tutors

For more advanced students, a couple of meetings with a tutor who specializes in English as a second language might be helpful. The tutor could identify your specific oral or written problems, work with you on a short-term basis, or recommend a course that would help you. To locate an ESL tutor, try calling the English as a second language department at a community college or university for recommendations. Private tutoring may be very expensive and difficult to find. You may also ask an educated English-speaking friend for language help.

Good First Step

Consider a visit to a public library in your area. A librarian can give you information about English books, tapes, CDs, Internet resources, and language classes offered locally. A few libraries even have language laboratories for language learners to use, as well as conversation classes.

QUICK REFERENCE

ESL Course Names

AE   American English or Academic English
EAL   English as an Additional Language
EAP   English for Academic Purposes
EFL   English as a Foreign Language (traditionally used abroad, in countries where English is not the first language)
EL   English Language
ESL   English as a Second Language
ESOL   English for/to Speakers of Other Languages
ESP   English for Specific Purposes (such as business English)
IESL   Intensive English as a Second Language
VESL   Vocational English as a Second Language (also VESEL)

Test Types

Academic Tests

Cambridge. Series of exams of British English, which certify English proficiency; the CPE is the Certificate of Proficiency in English; used in countries where British English is standard.

CELT. Comprehensive English Language Test; tests listening comprehension, structure, and vocabulary; given on-site by some colleges.

Michigan. Michigan Test of English Language Proficiency (MTELP); tests listening comprehension, grammar, vocabulary, and reading comprehension; given on-site by some colleges.

TAST. TOEFL Academic Speaking Test.

TOEFL. Test of English as a Foreign Language.

TSE. Test of Spoken English; given by the TOEFL company.

Tests Used for the Workplace, Adult Education, and Vocational Training

BEST. Basic English Skills Test; used for adults with limited English proficiency; used for vocational English programs.

CASAS. Comprehension Adult Student Assessment System; used in adult basic education and vocational English programs.

TOEIC. Test of English for International Communication; used by employers in the workplace; tests listening comprehension and reading comprehension.

RESOURCE DIRECTORY

How to Use This List

- The following list includes many, but not all, of the English as a Second Language (ESL) programs in the Washington area. Be aware that times, dates, offerings, and costs change frequently. The websites for the programs may provide you with useful information about levels, schedules, beginning dates, costs, etc. However, call the school for up-to-date information before beginning a language program.
- Brief annotations are given under the headings "Universities and Four-Year Colleges That Offer ESL Programs" and "Adult Education Programs."

Universities and Four-Year Colleges That Offer ESL Programs

Washington, D.C.

The Catholic University of America
Intensive English Program
324 Pangborn Hall
620 Michigan Avenue, NE
Washington, DC 20064
Phone: 202-319-4439 or 202-319-5229
Fax: 202-319-6032
english.cua.edu/IEP/
(Intensive programs in English for Academic Purposes; summer session offers shorter courses)

The George Washington University
801 22nd Street, NW, Academic Center 216
Washington, DC 20052
Phone: 202-994-6333
Fax: 202-994-8199
www.gwu.edu
E-mail: langlab@gwu.edu
(English for Academic Purposes)

Georgetown University
English as a Foreign Language Program
37th and O Streets, NW
(Mailing address: 481 ICC, Box 57 1054)
Washington, DC 20057
Phone: 202-687-5978
Fax: 202-687-1707
www.georgetown.edu/departments/efl
E-mail: eflgu@gunet.georgetown.edu
(Intensive English program; American Language and Culture; American Conversational English [summer]; Pre-MBA Business English; Business Administration and Professional English)

The Johns Hopkins University
Paul H. Nitze School of Advanced International Studies
ESL and American Studies
1740 Massachusetts Avenue, NW
Washington, DC 20036
Phone: 202-663-5716 (summer programs only)
Fax: 202-663-5656 (summer programs only)
www.sais-jhu.edu/summer
E-mail: sais.summer@jhu.edu
(Programs for incoming graduate students and international professionals)

University of the District of Columbia
ESL Program
Department of Languages and Communication Disorders
4200 Connecticut Avenue, NW
Washington, DC 20008
Phone: 202-274-5556
Fax: 202-274-5230
(English for Academic Purposes)

Maryland Suburbs

Howard University Continuing Education
The Language Institute
1100 Wayne Avenue, Suite 100
Silver Spring, MD 20910
Phone: 301-585-2295
Fax: 301-585-8911
www.con-ed.howard.edu
    click Language Institute
(Academic ESL; ESL for general communication)

University of Maryland—College Park
Maryland English Institute
1101 Holzapfel Hall
College Park, MD 20742
Phone: 301-405-8634
Fax: 301-314-9462

www.mei.umd.edu
E-mail: mei@umail.umd.edu
(Intensive English programs; programs for part-time students; online
ESL courses)

Northern Virginia Suburbs

George Mason University
English Language Institute, MSN-4C4
4400 University Drive
Fairfax, VA 22030
Phone: 703-993-3660
Fax: 703-993-3664
eli.gmu.edu
    click the "I" in ELI
E-mail: eli@gmu.edu
(Intensive English for Academic Purposes; programs for international
professionals, business and embassy personnel)

Community College Programs

Community colleges may offer "credit," academic-type English
courses, and noncredit English courses. The two different programs are
listed separately for each college below.

Maryland Suburbs

Anne Arundel Community College
Continuing Education & Workforce Development—ESL Program
101 College Parkway
Arnold, MD 21012
Phone: 410-777-2901
Fax: 410-777-2822
www.aacc.edu
    click Prospective Students
    click Continuing Education and Workforce Development
    click English as a Second Language
(Noncredit courses)

College of Southern Maryland
Continuing Education & Workforce Development—ESL Program
8730 Mitchell Road
(Mailing address: PO Box 910)
La Plata, MD 20646
Phone: 301-934-7765 (Information Center)
Fax: 301-934-7698
(Information Center located at the La Plata Campus, AD Building)
www.csmd.edu
E-mail: info@csmd.edu
(ESL classes offered only at Waldorf Campus)

Frederick Community College
ESL Program
7932 Opossumtown Pike
Frederick, MD 21702
Phone: 301-846-2558
www.frederick.edu
  click Student Services
  click English as a Second Language

Howard Community College
English & Foreign Language Division
ESL Program (Credit)
10901 Little Patuxent Parkway
Columbia, MD 21044
Phone: 410-772-4410
Fax: 410-772-4401
www.howardcc.edu/english/esl

Howard Community College
Continuing Education ESL Program
10650 Hickory Ridge Road
Columbia, MD 21044
Phone: 410-772-4088
Fax: 410-772-4986
www.howardcc.edu/coned/esl
(Noncredit courses)

Howard Community College
English Language Institute
10650 Hickory Ridge Road
Columbia, MD 21044
Phone: 410-772-4740
Fax: 410-772-4067
www.howardcc.edu/eli
E-mail: eli@howardcc.edu
(Intensive English Program; noncredit courses; credit given at Howard
Community College for advanced ESL courses)

Montgomery College—Germantown Campus
American English Language Program
20200 Observation Drive
Germantown, MD 20976
Phone: 301-444-1803, 301-353-7746
Fax: 301-353-7752
www.montgomerycollege.edu
    click Admissions
    click American English Language

Montgomery College—Rockville Campus
American English Language Program
51 Mannakee Street
Rockville, MD 20850
Phone: 301-251-7407, 301-251-7408
Fax: 301-251-7463
www.montgomerycollege.edu
    click Admissions
    click American English Language

Montgomery College—Takoma Park Campus
American English Language Program
7600 Takoma Avenue
Takoma Park, MD 20012
Phone: 301-650-1368, 301-650-1378
Fax: 301-650-1669
www.montgomerycollege.edu
    click Admissions
    click American English Language

Montgomery College
Non-Credit Language Program—ESL
Workforce Development and Community Education
51 Mannakee Street
Rockville, MD 20850
Phone: 301-251-7262, 301-251-7936
Fax: 301-251-7937
www.montgomerycollege.edu
   click Continuing Education
   click Schedule of Classes
   click English as a Second Language
(Noncredit courses; courses are given at Rockville, Germantown, and
Takoma Park Campuses and other locations in the county)

Prince George's Community College
Department of Language Studies—ESL Program
301 Largo Road
Largo, MD 20774
Phone: 301-322-0946
Fax: 301-386-7532
www.pgcc.edu
   click Academic Programs
   click Academic Departments
   click Language Studies
   click ESL

Northern Virginia Suburbs

Northern Virginia Community College—Alexandria Campus
Humanities and Social Sciences Division, Room AA252
ESL (Credit Program)
3001 N. Beauregard Street
Alexandria, VA 22311
Phone: 703-845-6233
Fax: 703-845-6186
www.nvcc.edu/alexandria/
   click Humanities & Social Sciences
   click English as a Second Language

Northern Virginia Community College—Alexandria Campus
Continuing Education & Workforce Development—ESL Program

3001 N. Beauregard Street
Alexandria, VA 22311
Phone: 703-845-6240, 703-845-6280
Fax: 703-845-6083
www.nvcc.edu/alexandria/community/ESL.html
(Noncredit courses)

Northern Virginia Community College—Annandale Campus
Languages & Literature Division—ESL (Credit Program)
8333 Little River Turnpike
Annandale, VA 22003
Phone: 703-323-3291
Fax: 703-323-2144
www.nvcc.edu/annandale/
    click International Students
    click English Language Requirements

Northern Virginia Community College—Annandale Campus
Continuing Education & Workforce Development—ESL Program
8333 Little River Turnpike
Annandale, VA 22003
Phone: 703-323-3323
Fax: 703-323-3399
www.nvcc.edu/annandale/continuing/esl/
(Noncredit courses)

Northern Virginia Community College—Loudoun Campus
Humanities—ESL Program
1000 Harry Flood Byrd Highway
Sterling, VA 20164
Phone: 703-450-2550
Fax: 703-404-7368
www.nvcc.edu/loudoun/
    click Admissions and Records
    click International Students

Northern Virginia Community College—Loudoun Campus
Continuing Education & Workforce Development—ESL Program

1000 Harry Flood Byrd Highway
Sterling, VA 20164
Phone: 703-450-2551, 703-450-2552
Fax: 703-450-2669
www.nvcc.edu/loudoun/continuing/esl
(Noncredit courses)

Northern Virginia Community College—Manassas Campus
ESL Program
6901 Sudley Road
Manassas, VA 20109
Phone: 703-257-6530
Fax: 703-257-6551
www.nvcc.edu/manassas
    point to Courses Offered
    click ESL
Northern Virginia Community College—Manassas Campus
Continuing Education & Workforce Development—ESL Program
6901 Sudley Road
Manassas, VA 20109
Phone: 703-257-6530
Fax: 703-257-6551
www.nvcc.edu/manassas
    click Continuing Education and Workforce Development
    click ESL/ESOL
(Noncredit courses)

Northern Virginia Community College—Woodbridge Campus
Communication and Humanities—ESL Program
15200 Neabsco Mills Road
Woodbridge, VA 22191
Phone: 703-878-5715
Fax: 703-878-5678
www.nvcc.edu/woodbridge

Northern Virginia Community College—Woodbridge Campus
Continuing Education & Workforce Development—ESL Program
15200 Neabsco Mills Road

Woodbridge, VA 22191
Phone: 703-878-5770
Fax: 703-670-0246
www.nvcc.edu/woodbridge/continuing
   click ESL
E-mail: ContEducWo@nvcc.edu
(Noncredit courses)

Private/Corporate Language Programs

Washington, D.C.

Berlitz Language Center
1050 Connecticut Avenue, NW
Washington, DC 20036
Phone: 202-331-1160
Fax: 202-331-0043
www.berlitz.com
E-mail: washingtondc.lc@berlitz.com

International Center for Language Studies, Inc.
727 15th Street, NW, Suite 400
Washington, DC 20005
Phone: 202-639-8800
Fax: 202-783-6587
www.ICLS.com
E-mail: english@icls.com

International Language Institute
4301 Connecticut Avenue, NW, #147
Washington, DC 20008
Phone: 202-362-2505
Fax: 202-686-5603
www.transemantics.com
E-mail: ili@transemantics.com

LADO International College
Georgetown Campus
2233 Wisconsin Avenue, NW
Washington, DC 20007

Phone: 202-223-0023
Fax: 202-337-1118
www.lado.com
E-mail: lado-dc@lado.com

Sacred Heart Adult Education Center
1621 Park Road, NW
Washington, DC 20010
Phone: 202-462-6499
Fax: 202-986-7747
E-mail: shadulted@hotmail.com

Sanz School
1720 I Street, NW
Washington, DC 20006
Phone: 202-872-4700
Fax: 202-872-9009
www.sanzschool.com

Spanish Education Development (SED) Center
1840 Kalorama Road, NW
Washington, DC 20009
Phone: 202-462-8848
Fax: 202-462-6886
www.sedcenter.com
E-mail: info@sedcenter.com
(Open to all nationalities; for low-income immigrants)

Maryland Suburbs

Berlitz Language Center
1413 Annapolis Road, Suite 200
Odenton, MD 21113
Phone: 410-672-3410
Fax: 410-672-2242
www.berlitz.com
E-mail: odenton.lc@berlitz.com

Berlitz Language Center
11300 Rockville Pike, Suite 911
Rockville, MD 20852
Phone: 301-770-7550, 301-770-7551
Fax: 301-231-9506
www.berlitz.com
E-mail: rockville.lc@berlitz.com

English House
26 N. Summit Avenue
Gaithersburg, MD 20877
Phone: 301-527-0600
Fax: 301-527-1128
www.englishhouseusa.com
E-mail: ehouse@toad.net

English Now! Inc.
4903 Montgomery Lane
Bethesda, MD 20814
Phone: 301-718-3575
Fax: 301-718-6466
www.english-now.com
E-mail: englishnow@erols.com

LADO International College
Silver Spring Campus
1400 Spring Street, Suite 250
Silver Spring, MD 20910
Phone: 301-565-5236
Fax: 301-565-2360
www.lado.com
E-mail: lado-ss@lado.com

Sanz School
8455 Colesville Road, 2nd Floor
Silver Spring, MD 20910
Phone: 301-608-2300

Fax: 301-608-0802
www.sanzschool.com

Northern Virginia Suburbs

Berlitz Language Center
2070 Chain Bridge Road, Suite 140
Vienna, VA 22182
Phone: 703-883-0646
Fax: 703-442-9327
www.berlitz.com
E-mail: tysonscorner.lc@na.berlitz.com

Diplomatic Language Services
English Language Institute
1901 N. Fort Myer Drive, Suite 600
Arlington, VA 22209
Phone: 703-243-7003
Fax: 703-351-7426
www.dls-inc.com
E-mail: english@dls-inc.com
(Mostly for students from abroad)

Eurocentres
101 N. Union Street, Suite 300
Alexandria, VA 22314
Phone: 703-684-1494
Fax: 703-684-1495
www.eurocentres.com
   click English
   click Washington
E-mail: alx-info@eurocentres.com
(Mostly for students from abroad)

inlingua, School of Languages
English Center
1901 N. Moore Street, Suite LL-01
Arlington, VA 22209
Phone: 703-527-7888
Fax: 703-527-9866

www.inlinguadc.com
E-mail: english@inlinguadc.com
(Mostly for students from abroad)

LADO International College
Arlington Campus
1550 Wilson Boulevard, Garden Level
Arlington, VA 22209
Phone: 703-524-1100
Fax: 703-524-7681
www.lado.com
E-mail: lado-ar@lado.com

Sanz School
6182 Arlington Boulevard
Falls Church, VA 22044
Phone: 703-237-6200
Fax: 703-237-5495
www.sanzschool.com
(Intensive ESL; ESL/Medical Assisting Program, combines both English and medical assisting)

Adult Education Programs

Washington, D.C.

Carlos Rosario International
Career Center & Public Charter School
1100 Harvard Street, NW
Washington, DC 20009
Phone: 202-234-6522
Fax: 202-234-6563
www.carlosrosario.org
(Free for residents of D.C.)

District of Columbia, State Education Agency
Adult Education
4200 Connecticut Avenue, NW
Washington, DC 20008

Phone: 202-274-7181
Fax: 202-274-7188
www.dcadultliteracy.org
   click Find an Adult Education Program
   click ESOL
E-mail: info@dcadultliteracy.org
(Several locations throughout the city; addresses, phone, and fax numbers on website)

Maryland Suburbs

Calvert County Public Schools
Adult Education Program
4105 Old Town Road
Huntingtown, MD 20639
Phone: 410-535-7382
Fax: 410-535-7383
www.calvertnet.k12.md.us
(Several locations; free)

Charles County Literacy Council
3795 Leonardtown Road
Waldorf, MD 20601
Phone: 301-870-5974
Fax: 301-870-9106
www.charlescountyliteracy.org
E-mail: ccliteracy@ccboe.com
(One-on-one tutoring)

Charles County Public Schools
Lifelong Learning Center
ESOL Program
12300 Vivian Adams Drive
Waldorf, MD 20601
Phone: 301-753-1774, 301-645-4549
Fax: 301-645-4863
(Website pending)

Frederick County Public Schools
Adult Education

Walkersville "B" Building
44 Frederick Street
Walkersville, MD 21793
Phone: 240-236-8450
Fax: 240-236-8451
www.fcps.org/
  click Curriculum
  click Adult Education
  click ESOL
E-mail: adult.ed@fcps.org

Literacy Council of Montgomery County
11701 Georgia Avenue, Lower Level
Wheaton, MD 20902
Phone: 301-942-9292
Fax: 301-949-5464
www.literacycouncilmcmd.org
E-mail: info@literacycouncilmcmd.org
(One-on-one tutoring or groups of two or three)

Literacy Council of Prince George's County
6532 Adelphi Road, Suite 101
Hyattsville, MD 20782
Phone: 301-699-9770
Fax: 301-699-9707
www.literacycouncil.org
E-mail: info@literacycouncil.org
(One-on-one tutoring)

Montgomery County Public Schools
Adult Education
Refugee Training Program
919 University Boulevard West
Silver Spring, MD 20901
Phone: 301-649-8050
(ESL classes for refugees and political asylees only; Certified Nursing
Assistant classes; free)

Montgomery County Public Schools
Adult ESOL and Literacy-GED Programs
12518 Greenly Street
Silver Spring, MD 20906
Phone: 301-929-6941
Fax: 301-929-2099
www.mcps.k12.md.us/curriculum/adultesol
(Locations throughout the county; beginning to intermediate levels, free, for county residents only; higher levels, tuition, open to residents of other counties)

Prince George's County Public Schools
Adult Basic Education—ESL
6111 Ager Road
Hyattsville, MD 20782
Phone: 301-408-7930
Fax: 301-408-7929
www.pgcps.org/~adult
    click English as a Second Language
E-mail: adult.ed@pgcps.org
(Locations throughout the county; lower-level courses, free; tuition for higher levels)

Prince George's County Public Schools
Adult Education
Refugee Training Program
5150 Annapolis Road
Bladensburg, MD 20710
Phone: 301-985-1808
Fax: 301-985-1794
www.pgcps.org/~adult
    click Refugee Training Program
(Free; for refugees and political asylees only)

Northern Virginia Suburbs

Alexandria City Public Schools
Alexandria Adult Learning Center
25 South Quaker Lane, Room 28

Alexandria, VA 22314
Phone: 703-461-4179
Fax: 703-751-2251
(Small fee for Alexandria residents; open to nonresidents for a higher
fee; daytime classes only)

Alexandria City Public Schools
Alexandria Community Education
3330 King Street
Alexandria, VA 22302
Phone: 703-824-6845
Fax: 703-824-6902
www.acps.k12.va.us/adultctr.php
E-mail: adulted@acps.k12.va.us
(Residents and nonresidents; locations throughout the county)

Arlington Public Schools Adult Education
Arlington Education and Employment Program (REEP)
2801 Clarendon Boulevard, Suite 218
Arlington, VA 22201
Phone: 703-228-4200
Fax: 703-527-6966
www.arlington.k12.va.us/departments/adulted/REEP
(Locations throughout the county)

Fairfax County Public Schools
Adult Education
Adult English for Speakers of Other Languages
7731 Leesburg Pike, Room 147A
Falls Church, VA 22043
Phone: 703-714-5560
Fax: 703-714-5589
www.fcps.edu/DIS/OACE/esol.htm
(Locations throughout the county; reduced tuition for residents of Fair-
fax County only)

Falls Church City Public Schools
Adult Education/Community Education Office

803 W. Broad Street, Suite 340
Falls Church, VA 22046
Phone: 703-248-5686
Fax: 703-248-5685
www.fccps.k12.va.us/html/comclass.htm#esl
(Free; students need photo ID)

Hogar Hispano (Catholic Charities)
6201 Leesburg Pike, Suite 307
Falls Church, VA 22044
Phone: 703-534-9805
Fax: 703-534-9809
www.ccda.net
    click Programs and Services
    click English as a Second Language
(Open to all immigrants; locations throughout Northern Virginia; regis-
tration fee includes tuition)

Literacy Council of Northern Virginia, Inc.
English as a Second Language
3431 Carlin Springs Road
Falls Church, VA 22041
Phone: 703-575-7900
Fax: 703-2317-2863, 703-575-6574
www.lcnv.org
E-mail: info@lcnv.org
(One-on-one tutoring and classes; class fee includes book, tutored stu-
dents buy books)

Prince William County Public Schools
Adult Education
PO Box 389
Manassas, VA 20108
Phone: 703-791-7357
Phone: 703-791-2319 (recorded message for locations, schedule)
Fax: 703-791-8889
www.pwcs.edu/pwc/adulted/eslpwcps.html

Professional Test Preparation Center

Kaplan Educational Centers, Inc.
Phone: 1-800-527-8378 (1-800-KAPTEST)
www.kaplaninternational.com
E-mail: world@kaplan.com
Kaplan Washington, D.C., Center
2025 M Street, NW
Washington, DC 20036
Phone: 202-835-9745
Fax: 202-296-5771
(Preparation for professional exams and licensing, e.g., medical; general intensive ESL; TOEFL and Academic English Preparation)

Some of the information in this list was based on entries that appeared in the *WATESOL Directory 2002*, a publication of The Washington Area Teachers of English for Speakers of Other Languages. For more information about this organization, the website is www.watesol.org.

Chapter Two

Discovering Your Career Options

As a new resident of the United States who wants to develop a career, you will want information on how to navigate the American labor market. You may have one or more of the following questions:

• How do I change my career to fit in the American labor market?
• How do I prepare myself to pursue this career?
• How do I use my foreign credentials to lead to a career?
• How do I find a job and succeed in my career?

Career counselors can assist you. These professionally trained individuals can guide you through the following career planning process:

1. Discovering yourself—assess and clarify your abilities, interests, values, skills, and preferences.
2. Finding options—identify occupations that fit your unique interests, strengths, and abilities.
3. Deciding and acting—list your objectives, initiate employment and educational strategies.

WHERE DO YOU FIND HELP?

You will find many resources for career help, advice, and job opportunities in the Washington metropolitan area. (The resource directory in this chapter focuses primarily on government agencies and educational institutions and provides examples of community organizations).

Government Agencies: Federal, State, and Local Resources

Employment, education, and training services are provided by state and local governments in partnership with the federal government through the "one-stop" concept—a single location that provides a variety of career services. Information is provided in person and electronically.

The public can obtain general career information electronically. Individuals who work with career counselors at one-stop centers can obtain tailored electronic feedback for their career needs. The one-stop concept is available in the District of Columbia, Maryland, and Virginia. Most services are free; however, some programs require residency and/or income eligibility.

Educational Institutions: Colleges and Universities

Colleges and universities provide information and services through well-equipped career information and resource centers, career counseling offices, and student employment services. Most career centers have computerized Career Information Delivery Systems (CIDS) and other sophisticated software programs for exploring careers. The centers also have electronic resources, Internet access, the latest books and publications, specialized job database systems, and assessment testing tools.

Students who are enrolled at these educational institutions have first priority at the career centers. Community members who do not take courses may gain limited access to services or may be required to pay for specialized services such as individual career counseling. Public universities have more liberal policies about community use than private schools; and two-year community colleges provide the most services to the community.

Community Organizations: Religious, Ethnic/Cultural, and Social Services

Community organizations usually focus their services on specific populations, such as serving only low-income residents, people with disabilities, older workers, the homeless, or ethnic/cultural groups. Volunteers usually provide skills training, counseling, and information and referral services. Locate community organizations through local churches, ethnic organizations, public libraries, and community directories.

Public Libraries

Public libraries offer traditional means of finding information, as well as Internet access. Public libraries are in every community, and most materials are free for you to use. Among other information, you can access directories of national trade and professional associations, guides to colleges and universities, journals, newspapers and magazines, books on particular careers, and information on international, national, and local companies as well as specialized online databases.

Private Career Counseling Agencies and Individual Practices

These private sources provide specialized services either in individual or group career counseling settings, as well as personal career coaching. Agencies and practices charge from $60 to $200 per one-hour session. You may want to obtain recommendations from two of the nationally recognized counseling associations listed in Appendix A.

Third-Party Recruiters

Third-party recruiters include agencies or individuals who contact candidates for temporary, part-time, or full-time employment. You may be contacted by search firms, temporary agencies, contract recruiters, and firms that offer to promote your resume. The company may charge you or the employer for its services. See Appendix A for possible associations to which third-party recruiters may belong. You may also want to do your own research to check on companies that contact you, if you are not familiar with them.

RESUMING YOUR PROFESSION

General Information

Become familiar with your profession/paraprofession as practiced in the United States. For employment trends in your profession, see websites at the end of this chapter; also watch for media coverage of employment trends. (For example, Developing Shortage of Dentists, National Public Radio feature, Thursday, February 27, 2003, at www .marketplace.org. Click Morning Report, click Show Archives, click February 27, 2003, 8:50 a.m. feed, which contains several subject areas. Discuss your findings on employment trends with a college financial aid counselor.

If you need a license to practice your profession, obtain licensing requirements from your state licensing board. If necessary, check to see whether your state accommodates political refugees who cannot obtain all documents. Get the most recent information from individual state boards or your professional association on how much of your foreign training and experience can be applied toward obtaining your U.S. license—you will probably need to get your foreign background evaluated (see appendix C). Check whether you need to retrain in your profession or whether evidence of your credentials and experience are acceptable.

Note: Do not attempt to evaluate the impact on your future of licensing requirements! Consult a career counselor to determine how complicated, long, and expensive it will be for you to earn your license, particularly if you are resuming the same profession you practiced outside the United States.

Opportunities Outside the Washington Region

You may decide to move from the Washington metropolitan area, either temporarily or permanently, for one or more of the following reasons:

- The retraining you need may be available in another part of the country, instead of the Washington metropolitan area (see appendix D).
- Licensing regulations and requirements may be more favorable to your background in another state. Check with your national association or another state licensing board. For example, the amount of time it takes for foreign-trained physicians to become licensed varies from state to state.
- There may be a greater need for your professional skills in another part of the country. Consult your professional national association.

Also check occupational projections, http://almis.dws.state.ut.us/occ/ projhome.asp.

- There may be more educational financial assistance available—or your loan repayment may be more favorable—in locations where there is a great need for certain professions. Examples of such professions include teachers in Maryland, nurses in the Washington, D.C., metropolitan area, and lawyers entering public service. Check financial aid websites for various states. See chapter four.

CAREERS RELATED TO YOUR PROFESSION

Become a Paraprofessional

A paraprofessional assists and is supervised by a professional. For example, a physician's assistant is a paraprofessional supervised by a physician, and a paralegal assists an attorney. To reduce retraining time, find out how much course credit you can receive for your foreign professional education and experience (see appendix C). Also, check requirements for licensing with the state licensing board that handles the paraprofession.

Retrain in a Related Field

Combine your education and experience for new careers that do not require lengthy retraining. For example, if you were an architect, you might pursue a career in interior design or landscape design.

NEW CAREER PATHS

Become an Entrepreneur

Start-up businesses often begin as home-based businesses. Determine what licenses and regulations apply. Investigate the advantages, risks, and liabilities of how you legally establish your business—you may not need to incorporate.

Also, know the difference between an independent contractor and an employee before you contract your services with a company or government agency. In some situations, you may be paid for your services as an employee, even if you do not think you are an employee working at the organization full-time or permanent part-time. Your risks, liabilities, obligations, and tax consequences differ for independent contractor and for employee. (See quick reference, independent contractor, employee.)

The following are ways to get more information and help:

Consult your county's economic development department. The department provides you with the path and phone numbers for opening your business. Also, inquire about sources of funds and loans, and local economic trends. The department often presents helpful seminars and networking opportunities. The department may have no-cost mentors for start-up businesses, as well as business counselors who can give you advice and referrals.

Contact the Small Business Development Center (SBDC) in your area. Funded by the U.S. Small Business Administration (SBA), SBDCs provide education, training, and business counseling for you to develop a business plan, to identify funding sources, and to help resolve engineering and technical problems. SBDCs may be affiliated with colleges and universities. Also, consult the Entrepreneurship Center for New Americans (ECNA) at the Business Development Assistance Group. This unique center is partly funded by the U.S. Small Business Administration specifically to focus on the business and professional needs of immigrants.

Attend chamber of commerce monthly networking meetings or events. Almost every jurisdiction (county or city) in the region has at least one chamber of commerce, so there is an abundance of chambers in the Washington region, both large and small. Call to ask whether you can attend as a guest (free) once or twice. Ask the public library reference desk for a list of chambers of commerce.

Consult the high-technology council in your location, if your idea is technology related. Examples are Northern Virginia Technology Council, Fauquier Technology Alliance, and Maryland High Technology Council.

Take a noncredit course at your local community college on starting a business. A course familiarizes you with American business practices. These are short, inexpensive courses offered by the college's continuing education department (see chapter 3), sometimes in conjunction with the U.S. Small Business Administration.

Contact private consultants who specialize in business development. You may obtain names in several ways, in addition to personal referral: contact the department of business administration of a university, an SBDC, or your local chamber of commerce. Ask these organizations what credentials to look for in a business consultant. Check with the Better Business Bureau and the government consumer affairs department in your area for any possible complaints about such private consultants (see appendix A).

Use online help for general information. For excellent general online information and help on starting a business, check www.SBA.gov.

Retrain in Information Technology

If you have strong analytical skills and related aptitudes, you may want a career in information technology—perhaps combining IT with your previous professional background. For example, if you were a legal professional in your native country, you might work in a large law firm as a network engineer. Or if you were a medical professional in your native country, you might work in a hospital, university medical center, managed care facility, or medical insurance company as a network engineer. Consider that if American English fluency is a concern for you, network engineers, as well as programmers and analysts, may not need advanced English skills.

There are fast-paced computer training programs for recareering professionals. Check with your local community college and private educational technology institutions. Also, contact community-based organizations; they may offer or be planning to offer reduced-cost programs to retrain professionals in high technology.

Investigate a New Career Interest

Here are some ways to explore potential career interests:

- Work with a career counselor to discuss your skills as applicable to a new field and to discuss employment trends. A career counseling professional will guide you through the career process and provide you with follow-up resources. To locate help, see the beginning of this chapter and the resource directory.
- Consider networking to ask about new careers.
- Schedule an informational interview with a high-ranking professional or entrepreneur at a government agency or a company. Through the informational interview format, you exchange ideas

with a professional or entrepreneur in his or her work environment, to determine how your background would be received by others in the field and to explore job opportunities or mentorships in the profession. The informational interview is not an interview for a job with a particular company. Its success depends on the goodwill of the professional or entrepreneur you select and want to interview. A career counselor can help you prepare for the informational interview.

OTHER RESOURCES

First Steps

1. Familiarize yourself with employment trends and how they are related to your skills—both in the Washington region and around the country.
2. Discuss your background with career counselors and professionals in your new field of interest.
3. Determine how much time would be required for you to complete the process of changing fields—from retraining to licensing to employment.
4. Explore fast-track retraining programs.
5. Check entrepreneurship opportunities

Books

Bolles, Richard Nelson. *What Color Is Your Parachute? A Practical Manual for Job Hunters and Career Changers*. Berkeley, Calif.: Ten Speed Press, 2003. Published annually, this is a standard resource for individuals and career professionals who are counseling individuals.

Haldane, Bernard Associates, Inc. *Haldane's Best Answers to Tough Interview Questions*. Manassas Park, Va.: Impact Publications, 2000. Covers interview techniques from preparation to follow up and gives samples of key questions and answers.

Krannich, Ronald, and William J. Banis. *High Impact Resumes and Letters: How to Communicate Your Qualifications to Employers*. 8th ed. Manassas, Va.: Impact Publications, 2002.

National Trade and Professional Associations of the United States. 37th ed. Washington, D.C.: Columbia Books, 2003. This directory lists over 5,000 associations. It also contains websites for career searches.

Occupational Outlook Handbook 2002–3. Washington, D.C.: U.S. Department of Labor, Bureau of Labor Statistics, 2002. Annual publication.

Websites

Some of the Internet sites may charge for services such as posting resumes, career assessments, and counseling; however, there are plenty of free services. Also take note of resume databases that may not be secure.

Career Searches

America's Career InfoNet. (www.acinet.org) Provides information on options for work and learning skills required for different occupations, identification of employers, resources for job search, and educational and training resources. This site features its own career resource library that has a comprehensive list of resources and links.

The Occupational Outlook Handbook (OOH) On-Line. (http://stats.bls.gov/oco/home.htm) The site is compiled by the U.S. Bureau of Labor Statistics. It provides data on specific careers: nature of the job, working conditions, employment outlook, training requirements, earnings, and other related information. The print version is recognized nationally as a source of career information and has been a standard resource in college and university career centers.

O*NET: Occupational Information Network Resource Center. (www.onetcenter.org/) The system is an electronic revision and update of the *Dictionary of Occupational Titles.* Maintained by the U.S. Department of Labor as a major career reference, the site uses data to support career exploration and job searching.

O*NET. (http://online.onetcenter.org) O*NET OnLine leads you to the O*NET database, which is an interactive database for skills, abilities, knowledge, interests, and work activities.

Job Hunters Bible. (www.jobhuntersbible.com) The site is a supplement to the book *What Color Is Your Parachute* by Richard Bolles. The book is widely used by career professionals particularly to advise individuals on career changing and job search. The website provides five headings—job listings, resumes, career counseling, research, and networking.

CareerBuilder. (www.CareerBuilder.com) A huge site for career building, it provides a job search database, salary wizard, resume and interview tips, and career counseling information. It provides links for career assessments, coaching and counseling, as well as job placement.

What Can I Do with a Major in . . . (www.uncwil.edu/stuaff/career/majors) An excellent site to help you translate your major into an occupation or career. The information includes related career titles for each occupation, job skills related to the academic major, and useful links. "What Can I Do with a Major in . . .?" is an appropriate title for this site.

Job Searches

America's Job Bank. (www.ajb.org) This is a service of the U.S. Department of Labor with links to state employment offices and to federal job openings. There is a free service that connects job seekers and employers through a nationwide resume database that allows a search by job title, occupation, location, and wages.

Riley Guide. (www.rileyguide.com) This site is authored by Margaret Riley, respected author of the book *The Guide to Internet Job Searching*. The site provides information on how to use the Internet for job searches and on how to find other resources on the Internet.

Monster Board. (www.monster.com) This site provides information on national and international jobs, career fairs, resume connection and job search by location, category, and company name, articles on careers, as well as company websites. It links to www.jobprofiles.com, which provides practical information on occupations listed by common job names.

Job Hunt. (www.job-hunt.org) One of the most comprehensive sites. It features a well-organized list of job-related sites and job search by location, category, and profession/industry. It also provides links to useful job resources.

Career Journal. (www.careerjournal.com) Information from the *Wall Street Journal,* the *National Business Employment Weekly,* is on this site. There is also a database for middle-level to senior-level positions, as well as an electronic librarian, and access to a salary search.

Career Journal. (www.jobstar.org) At this site you will find information on resume and cover-letter writing, as well as thank-you letters. It sections include "Guides for Careers" and "The Hidden Job Market."

The Industry Masterlist. (http://hoovers.com/) The site provides a reference for over 300 industries divided into twenty-eight sectors.

Salary Wizard. (www.salary.com) One of the most popular salary-comparison sites. The Salary Wizard allows a search by job category and region, as well as a quick search for median salaries by position. See also www.bls.gov/oes/2001/oessrcst.htm.

QUICK REFERENCE

Alternative Career Examples

Alternative Careers for Accountants

Here are several sets of alternatives if you do not choose to become a certified public accountant (CPA). You will certainly add more options.

Alternative 1. Focus on other accounting opportunities that do not need licensing in the Washington region. In Maryland, the District of Columbia, and Virginia, only CPAs must be licensed. Other accountants are: public accounting (PA), registered public accountants (RPA), accounting practitioners (AP), management accountants, internal auditors, and government accountants and auditors.

Alternative 2. Apply your accounting specialty or subspecialty to another profession or career, either temporarily or permanently. A few examples are purchasing agent (if you have a background in evaluating contracts), insurance agent (if you have a background in insurance dealings), stock broker (if you have a background in financial planning), financial planner or manager, insurance underwriter, customers broker, actuary, and real estate broker.

Alternative 3. Retrain as a computer analyst/programmer, thus using your analytical and reasoning skills and comfort with numbers to find high-paying jobs for which you can receive training quickly.

Here are some professional associations and organizations to contact:

Institute of Management Accountants, 10 Paragon Drive, Montvale, NJ 07645, Phone: 201-573-9000, 800-638-4427, Fax: 201-474-1600, www.imanet.org, E-mail: cmacfm@imanet.org (CMA information)

National Society of Accountants, www.nsacct.org, Phone: 703-549-6400, Accreditation Council for Accountancy & Taxation: www.acatcredentials, Org phone: 703-549-2228, 1010 N. Fairfax Street, Alexandria, VA 22314, Fax: 703-549-2984 (Business accountant, tax advisor, tax preparer accreditations)

Career Options
Quick Reference

The Institute of Internal Auditors, 247 Maitland Avenue, Altamonte Springs, FL 32701-4201, Phone: 407-937-1100, www.theiia.org (CIA designation)

For a list of schools in accounting and business, contact: American Assembly of Collegiate Schools of Business, 600 Emerson Road, St. Louis, MO 63141, Phone: 314-872-8481, Fax: 314-872-8495, www.aacsb.edu (Accredited programs in accounting and business)

Also, check appendix D for all academic programs throughout the United States.

Alternative Careers for Engineers

Here are several sets of alternatives if you do not choose to become a licensed engineer. You will certainly add more options.

Alternative 1. Work as an engineer in a business, government, or nonprofit setting that does not require a professional engineer (PE) license. Ask the state licensing board for your state or the National Society of Professional Engineers for guidelines.

Alternative 2. Focus on other career opportunities using your analytical skills, such as computer and information systems manager, mathematician, computer systems engineers and scientists. Become involved in testing equipment or work in a research lab.

Alternative 3. Use your subspecialty in a technician capacity. Certification is voluntary and provided by the National Institute for Certification in Engineering Technologies (NICET). Engineering technician positions exist in the following engineering areas: civil, electrical and electronics, electromechanical, industrial, mechanical, chemical. Check on others.

Alternative 4. Retrain as a computer analyst/programmer, thus using your analytical and reasoning skills to find high-paying jobs for which you can receive training quickly.

Paraprofessional association to contact: The National Institute for Certification in Engineering Technologies, 1420 King Street, Alexandria, VA 22314, Phone: 888-IS-NICET, www.nicet.org

List of schools with accredited engineering technology programs: Accreditation Board for Engineering and Technology, Inc., 111 Market Place, Baltimore, MD 21202, Phone: 410-347-7700, Fax: 410-625-2238, www.abet.org

Alternative Careers for Health Professionals

Here are several sets of alternatives if you do not choose to return to your previous health profession. You will certainly add more options.

Alternative 1. You may want to work for a local biotechnology company. For a current list of biotech companies, use www.referenceusa.com through your public library, since this is a subscription database. The database will describe what the company does, its size, the name of the officers, along with the company's address and phone number. *or* You may want to teach in your field at a local community college, if you speak fluent English.

Alternative 2. Apply your profession or medical subspecialty to a related career, either temporarily while preparing to become licensed in your previous profession, or permanently. Here are some examples:

cardiologist	becomes	nurse practitioner cardiologist
pediatrician	becomes	pediatric physician's assistant
nurse practitioner	becomes	licensed practical nurse

Alternative 3. Select a paraprofession. There are many, including:

diagnostic medical sonographer	health information technologist	nuclear medical technician
physical therapist assistant	emergency medical technician	nursing assistant
medical assistant	cardiovascular technologist	dental assistant
phlebotomist	surgical technologist	pharmacy technician/assistant
dental hygienist	lab technician	licensed practical nurse
radiologic technologist	home health aide	physician assistant

Alternative 4. Retrain as a computer analyst/programmer, thus using your analytical and reasoning skills in a high-paying job for which you can receive training quickly. *or* Investigate an entirely new field you have always wanted to consider.

Here are some selected paraprofessional associations:

American Academy of Physician Assistants, 950 N. Washington Street, Alexandria, VA 22314, Phone: 703-836-2272, Fax: 703-684-1924, www.aapa.org

American Dental Assistants Association, 35 E. Wacker Drive, Chicago, IL 60601, Phone: 312-541-1550, Fax: 312-541-1496, www.dentalassistant.org

American Dental Hygienists Association, 444 N. Michigan Avenue, Chicago, IL 60611, Phone: 312-440-8900, Fax: 312-467-1806, www.adha.org

For certification information—clinical laboratory technologists and technicians:

American Association of Bioanalysts, 917 Locust Street, St. Louis, MO 63101, Phone: 314-241-1445, Fax: 314-241-1449, www.aab.org

American Medical Technologists, 710 Higgins Road, Park Ridge, IL 60068, Phone: 847-823-5169, 800-275-1268, Fax: 847-823-0458, www.amt1.com

American Society for Clinical Laboratory Science, 6701 Democracy Boulevard, Bethesda, MD 20817, Phone: 301-657-2768, Fax: 301-564-9619, www.ascls.org

American Society for Clinical Pathology, 2100 W. Harrison Street, Chicago, IL 60612, Phone: 312-738-1336, Fax: 312-738-5808, www.ascp.org

American Society of Cytopathology, 400 W. Ninth Street, Suite 201, Wilmington, DE 19801, Phone: 302-429-8802, Fax: 302-429-8807, www.cytopathology.org

Check appendix D for academic programs throughout the United States.

Certification and Licensure Definition

Certification. Certification is written proof of your qualifications, such as completion of a course. Certification can have several applications:

- Occupational certification by a government body: Certification is government recognition of a person's qualifications. Certification may not have as many requirements as licensing and is often optional. For example, interior designers in Maryland can be state certified, but the State of Maryland does not *require* certification to practice as an interior designer.
- Occupational certification by a private organization, business or professional association, or educational institution: This type of certification is an organization's recognition that an individual has met certain educational standards. For example, LERN (Learning Resources Network, www.lern.org) provides Certified Program Planner (CPP) certification to individuals who have completed its training program.

Individuals may find certification a useful additional career credential. *Note:* In some old laws, the term *certification* is used interchangeably with *licensing.*

Licensing (or licensure). Certain professions and occupations require licenses in the United States. A license is a credential awarded to an individual who meets a set of standards set by a government body called a licensing board. The license represents the government's formal review, approval of qualifications, and authorization to practice a profession or occupation. The approval process is called licensure. (An individual who holds a professional or occupational license is accountable to the government body for his or her actions.)

Licensure of professions is managed by state governments. Therefore, in many professions, *licenses are granted by each state* where you want to practice, rather than by the federal government. For example, if you are licensed in Georgia as an attorney, you cannot practice in New Hampshire unless you obtain a New Hampshire license. License requirements will probably vary from state to state.

Independent Contractor and Employee Definition

Source: Friedman, Jack. *Barron's Dictionary of Business Terms.* 3d ed. Barron's Educational Series, Inc., 2000.

> [A]n *Independent Contractor* makes an agreement to do a specific piece of work, retaining control of the means and methods of doing the job; neither

party has the right to terminate the contract at will. . . . Federal income taxes and Social Security taxes are not withheld by employers of independent contractors; independent contractors are subject to self-employment tax. (pp. 140–41)

[An] *Employee* [is a] person who works for compensation, whether direct or indirect, for another in return for stipulated services. An employee may work on an hourly, daily, or annual wage basis. The *employer* has the right to control the work to be performed as well as the timing and means of accomplishing the work. (p. 217)

Licensing Steps

Occupations That Often Require Licensing

Health, legal, and accounting (CPA) professions require licensing. Engineers dealing with the public in their own practices must be licensed. In addition, the following professions and occupations often require a state license. This is not a comprehensive list; check with the individual state.

real estate appraiser	barber	funeral director
land surveyor	interior designer	plumber
architect	veterinarian	steam and other operating engineer
boxing and wrestling official	dental hygienist	security guard
electrician	financial planner	emergency medical technician
real estate broker	insurance agent	optometrist
social worker	psychologist	real estate broker
stock broker	geologist	land surveyor
polygraph examiner	soil scientist	home improvement contractor
home inspector	pawnbroker	sports agent
pilot	auctioneer	cosmetologist

Elements You Need to Become Licensed

Some or all of the following elements are required to qualify you for a license, depending on the profession and the state where you want to obtain your license:

- Education in the field
- Internships, supervised practical experience, preclinical or clinical requirement

- Credentials evaluation, including education and experience
- References check
- Licensing exam
- Payment of fees
- Social security number
- Citizenship or visa status
- Copy of your previous license
- Photo identification of yourself

Licensing Process

1. Contact the state agency for your profession. The state agency is usually called the "state licensing board." See the Resource Directory, "Examples of Licensing Contacts." Ask to receive the application for licensure, including both (1) licensing requirements and (2) special procedures for foreign-trained professionals if there are such procedures.

2. Contact the association for your profession. Get the association name from the state licensing board or check the *Encyclopedia of Associations* at the public library. Your professional association can provide much of the following information:

- Job trends and job opportunities in your field
- Foreign-trained professionals committee, if there is one within the association
- Attitudes toward foreign-trained professionals in the profession and with the public
- Nationwide licensing developments for foreign-trained professionals, such as state reciprocity if you are already licensed in one state, or substitution of qualifications
- Resources, courses, and materials available to prepare for the licensing exam
- Local association chapter with phone number, website, address, and contact person

As an example of information provided by an association, here is what the American Dental Association offers at www.ada.org/prof/prac/licensure/lic-intl.html. We gratefully acknowledge the American Dental Association for permission to use this information.

Dentistry in the United States
Information on Education and Licensure
CONTENTS

Admission to the United States 1
Dental Licensure 2
Basic Dental Education 5
Advanced Dental Education 7
Other Educational Opportunities 9
Opportunities for Employment 13
American Dental Association 14
APPENDIX A: State Boards of Dentistry: Information on Educational
                Statutory and Regulatory Provisions 15
APPENDIX B: Accredited Dental Schools That Accept International
                Dental Graduates with Advanced Standing 16
APPENDIX C: Advanced Dental Education Programs that Have in
                the Past Considered Admitting Graduates of
                International Dental Schools 18
APPENDIX D: Step-by-Step to Dental Licensure in the United States
                for International Dental Graduates 22
APPENDIX E: State and Regional Clinical Dental Testing Agencies 24

---

3. Meet licensing requirements set by the state licensing board for your state. When you are ready for your licensing exam, your state board will let you know whether you must schedule your licensing exam through the state board or on your own.

There are often review courses, as well as books and tapes, to help you prepare for the licensing exam. Your state licensing board or your national association will guide you. They may even provide sample questions for the licensing exam.

Here are additional ideas on how to study for your licensing exam:

- Talk with professionals in your field about available resources.
- Attend an intensive test preparation class. Such classes may be provided by commercial companies. For example, Barbri Bar Review (www.barbri.com) provides such classes for lawyers taking state licensing exams.
- Audit a class in your profession to review American terminology and practice.
- Talk with faculty members at a local college or university.

- Take the initiative to develop an informal, brief mentorship through your contacts with area professionals or through your professional association.

4. Pay fees. Fees that usually apply are license application fee, exam fee, and license fee.

World of Associations in the U.S.

In no country in the world has the principle of association been more successfully used or applied to a greater multitude of objects than in America . . .

An association consists simply in the public assent which a number of individuals give to certain doctrines and in the engagement which they contract to promote in a certain manner the spread of those doctrines.
— Alexis de Tocqueville, *Democracy in America*

What Is the Importance of Associations for You?

Being exposed to or involved with an association is an important way for you to learn how your profession or potential field is practiced in the United States, and a way for you to network—make personal contacts with individuals in your field. In addition, you may discover specialties and subspecialties in your field you had not previously considered practicing in the United States. Finally, when you belong to an established and reputable professional association or organization in your field, you are adding a credential to your resume, since employers and the general public are aware that associations set standards that members must follow.

What Is the Role of Associations in the United States?

Professional and trade (business and commerce) associations play an important role in the United States and are very common. An association consists of a group of people in one professional area or one type of business who come together as a nonprofit membership organization.

There are often dues to maintain the organization. Here are some activities of associations:

- Provide networking opportunities for members through meetings and special conferences, so they can know each other through personal contact; this is one key reason professionals and businesspersons join an association
- Establish professional requirements to practice in the field and cooperate with state licensing boards, where applicable
- Establish ethical standards for its members
- Keep members up to date on developments, regulations, and research in the field through newsletters, other publications, seminars, and conferences
- Maintain job opportunity referrals through hotlines, websites, or other means
- Promote members' areas of interest to the general public
- Provide members with information on licensing requirements and board exams or certification and updated training, where applicable
- Lobby government agencies on issues of importance to members

What Types of Associations Are There?

There are national associations in many fields. Such organizations may also have chapters in your state and local geographic area; you can probably locate state and local chapters through the national association website. In a particular field, there also may be independent associations not specifically affiliated with the national association. Examples of national organizations are American Bar Association, American Dental Association, American Medical Association, American Institute of Certified Public Accountants, and American Nurses Association. Examples of trade associations are National Association of Manufacturers, National Rifle Association, American Bankers Association.

In addition to large national associations, there are also smaller associations that focus on specialties within a field or specific ethnic groups' interests. As a result professionals and businesspersons often belong to more than one association.

How Can You Find an Association in Your Field?

Locate Reference Information. Available at your public library reference desk:

Encyclopedia of Associations. 39th ed. Detroit: Gale, 2003. *Associations Unlimited* is the online database; it is probably available through your public library.
National Trade and Professional Associations of the United States. 37th ed. Washington, D.C.: Columbia Books, 2003.

Also search American Society of Association Executives' website: asaenet.org. Click Find, People, Associations and Businesses, click Gateway to Associations, then put in key words.

Search Creatively for Small, Informal Associations. While large associations are formal with offices and staffs, very small and informal associations may have no office or no phone listing and may be difficult to find. Here are a few ways to locate small, informal associations:

• Ask a practitioner, business, or institution in your field of interest what are the associations in their field.
• Contact a newspaper reporter or publisher who covers your area of interest.
• For ethnic associations (for example, an association of Hispanic attorneys), ask the local chapter of the mainstream national professional association; ask the publisher of an ethnic newspaper (which you can often pick up at an ethnic restaurant or grocery); ask the publisher of a local mainstream community newspaper; ask a businessman whose shop is in an ethnic community within the Washington region; ask the director of an ethnic community center; ask the public library reference desk.

Examples of Associations in One Field

The following list of nurses associations gives you an example in just one field of how many targeted and specialized associations and organizations there might be. You may want to consider investigating the types of organizations or associations in your own field, and/or ask about special interest groups in the major national association for your field. We gratefully acknowledge the American Nurses Association for permission to use the following list from nursingworld.org/affil//index.htm:

Academy of Medical-Surgical Nurses
Air and Surface Transport Nurses
American Academy of Ambulatory Care Nursing
American Assembly for Men in Nursing
American Association for Continuity of Care
American Association of Critical-Care Nurses
American Association of Legal Nurse Consultants
American Association of Neuroscience Nurses
American Association of Nurse Anesthetists
American Association of Nurse Attorneys
American Association of Occupational Health Nurses
American Association of Spinal Cord Injury Nurses
American College of Nurse Practitioners
American Heart Association Council on Cardiovascular Nursing
American Holistic Nurses Association
American Medical Informatics Association
American Nephrology Nurses Association
American Nurses Association (national organization for all nurses)
American Psychiatric Nurses Association
American Public Health Association
American Radiological Nurses Association
American Society for Parenteral and Enteral Nutrition
American Society of Ophthalmic Registered Nurses, Inc.
American Society of Plastic and Reconstructive Surgical Nurses,
   Inc.
American Society of PeriAnesthesia Nurses
American Thoracic Society
Association for Child & Adolescent Psychiatric Nurses, Inc.
Association of Black Nursing Faculty in Higher Education, Inc.
Association of Community Health Nursing Educators
Association of Occupational Health Professionals
Association of Nurses in AIDS Care
Association of PeriOperative Registered Nurses, Inc.
Association of Pediatric Oncology Nurses
Association of Rehabilitation Nurses
Association of State and Territorial Directors of Nursing
Association of Women's Health, Obstetric, and Neonatal Nurses (for-
   merly NAACOG)

Chi Eta Phi Sorority
Consolidated Association of Nurses in Substance Abuse International
Council on Graduate Education for Administration in Nursing
Dermatology Nurses Association
Developmental Disabilities Nurses Association
Drug and Alcohol Nursing Association, Inc.
Emergency Nurses Association
Hospice Nurses Association
International Nurses Society on Addictions (formerly called National
    Nurses Society on Addictions)
International Society of Nurses in Genetics
International Society of Psychiatric Mental Health Nurses
Intravenous Nurses Society
National Association of Clinical Nurse Specialists
National Association of Directors of Nursing Administration in
Long Term Care
National Association of Hispanic Nurses
National Association of Neonatal Nurses
National Association of Nurse Massage Therapists
National Association of Nurse Practitioners in Reproductive Health
National Association of Orthopaedic Nurses
National Association of Pediatric Nurse Associates and Practitioners
National Association of School Nurses, Inc
National Association of State School Nurse Consultants, Inc.
National Black Nurses Association, Inc.
National Gerontological Nursing Association
National League for Nursing
National Nurses Society on Addictions (See: International Nurses Society on Addictions)
National Nursing Staff Development Organization
National Organization of Nurse Practitioner Faculties
National Student Nurses Association
North American Nursing Diagnosis Association
Nurses Organization of Veterans Affairs
Oncology Nursing Society
Philippine Nurses Association of America, Inc.
Respiratory Nursing Society
Sigma Theta Tau, International, Inc.

Society for Vascular Nursing
Society of Gastroenterology Nurses and Associates, Inc.
Society of Otorhinolaryngology and Head-Neck Nurses, Inc.
Society of Pediatric Nurses
Society of Urologic Nurses & Associates Inc.
Wound, Ostomy & Continence Nurses Society

RESOURCE DIRECTORY

How to Use This List

- This is not a comprehensive list. Check your local community for additional career guidance sites.
- Universities and colleges may require you to be enrolled as a student to use their facilities.
- Schools within universities may have their own career centers—law, business, others.
- If you cannot access the website listed, access the main website by eliminating forward slashes. Example: www.trinitydc.edu/current/career/index.html becomes www.trinitydc.edu. You can then identify the location you want to reach from the main page and left-click your mouse to get there.

Career Guidance

Washington, D.C.

The Washington, D.C., Department of Employment Services (DOES) is at 222.does.dc.gov/main.shtm. DOES provides employment and career-related services through one-stop centers listed below, and also through DC NetWorks—a virtual one-stop center that provides online career counselors, online job placement, and online training and education information. www.does.dc.gov/info/doescen.shtm

City Employment Services—General:

CVS Pharmacy/South Capitol
4049 S. Capitol Street, SW

Washington, DC 20032
Phone: 202-645-4000
Fax: 202-645-0022
www.does.dc.gov

Euclid Street One Stop Career Center
1704 Euclid Street, NW
Washington, DC 20009
Phone: 202-671-2940
Fax: 202-671-4093
www.does.dc.gov

Franklin Street Center
1500 Franklin Street, NE
Washington, DC 20018
Phone: 202-576-3091
TTY: 202-576-8128
Fax: 202-576-3100, 202-576-3109
www.does.dc.gov

Judiciary Square
441 Fourth Street, Ground Level, NW
Washington, DC 20001
Phone: 202-727-9726, 202-727-9727
TTY: 202-727-6714
Fax: 202-727-1334
www.docs.dc.gov

Metropolitan Washington Career Path Project
A. Philip Randolph Worker Center
6210 N. Capitol Street, NW
Washington, DC 20011
Phone: 202-576-6515
Fax: 202-576-3262
www.does.dc.gov

Naylor Road One-Stop Career Center
2626B Naylor Road, SE
Washington, DC 20020

Phone: 202-645-3535, press 9, ask for Naylor Road Center
TTY: 202-645-0019
Fax: 202-645-3073
www.does.dc.gov

Senior Programs—Government and Community Agencies:

District of Columbia, Office on Aging
Senior Service Network of Programs, Older Workers Employment
One Judiciary Square
441 Fourth Street, NW, Suite 900 S
Washington, DC 20001
Phone: 202-724-5622
Fax: 202-724-4979
www.dcoa.dc.gov/main.shtm

Forty Plus of Greater Washington DC
1718 P Street, NW
Washington, DC 20036
Phone: 202-387-1582
Fax: 202-387-7669
www.40plus-dc.org/
E-mail: info@40plusdc.org
(A nonprofit and dues-based membership organization that provides
self-help support and networking services to professionals who are at
the managerial level and are looking for new careers and/or jobs.)

National Association of Older Workers Employment Services
c/o National Council on the Aging
409 Third Street, SW, Suite 200
Washington, DC 20024
Phone: 202-479-1200, recording, press 0 and talk to operator
Fax: 202-479-0735
www.ncoa.org
www.ncoa.org/content.cfm?sectionID=38
E-mail: info@ncoa.org

National Caucus and Center on Black Aged, Inc. (55+)
1220 L Street NW, Suite 800

Washington, DC 20005
Phone: 202-637-8400
Fax: 202-347-0895
www.ncba-aged.org/
E-mail: info@ncba-aged.org

SeniorNet Learning Centers (computer learning centers for older workers)
SeniorNet Verizon Technology Center at UDC
4340 Connecticut Avenue, NW
Washington, DC 20008
Phone: 202-274-6670
www.seniornet.org/usa/washingtondc/

SeniorNet Chevy Chase Pavillion
5335 Wisconsin Avenue, NW
Washington, DC 20015
Phone: 202-237-7747
www.seniornet.org/usa/washingtondcnw/

Specialized Centers and Community Agencies:

People without Borders
3920 Alton Place, NW
Washington, DC 20016
Phone: 202-237-5711
Fax: 202-237-5711
www.peoplewithoutborders.org/
E-mail: info@peoplewithoutborders.org
(A nonprofit, Christian organization that recruits church volunteers from
area churches to provide services that empower immigrants and others in
the international community. Services provided include support network,
language skills, small business advice, and employment information.)

Washington DC Employment Support Center
1556 Wisconsin Avenue, NW
Washington, DC 20007
Phone: 202-628-2919
Fax: 202-628-2920

www.angelfire.com/biz/jobclubs/
jobclubs@hotmail.com
(The center is an example of a nonprofit, membership dues-based job club. It offers networking and other resources for job seekers. The services target professionals in the higher income level and include job club meetings, job bank, career library, and Internet services.)

Wider Opportunities for Women (WOW)
1001 Connecticut Avenue, NW, Suite 930
Washington, DC 20036
Phone: 202-464-1596
Fax: 202-464-1660
www.wowonline.org/
E-mail: info@wowonline.org
(A community organization that operates on volunteer help and community donations to support women and girls become economically self sufficient. WOW offers assistance for training, job placement, and business skills development.)

College and University Career Centers:

American University Career Center
Butler Pavilion
4400 Massachusetts Avenue, NW
Washington, DC 20016
Phone: 202-885-1804
Fax: 202-885-1861
www.american.edu/careercenter/
E-mail: careercenter@american.edu

The Catholic University of America
Career Center
202 Pryzbyla Center
620 Michigan Avenue, NE
Washington, DC 20064
Phone: 202-319-5623
Fax: 202-319-4480
careers.cua.edu/
E-mail: careers@cua.edu

Gallaudet University
Career Center
800 Florida Avenue, NE
Washington, DC 20002
Phone: 202-651-5355, 202-651-5449
TTY: 202-651-5441
careercenter.gallaudet.edu/

The George Washington University
Career Center
1922 F Street, NW
Washington, DC 20052
Phone: 202-994-6495
Fax: 202-994-6493
www.gwu.edu./~fellows/career.html
E-mail: gwcarctr@gwu.edu

Georgetown University
MBNA Career Education Center
37th and O Streets, NW
One Leavey Center, Box 571086
Washington, DC 20057
Phone: 202-687-3493
Fax: 202-687-8519
careerweb.georgetown.edu/

Howard University
Career Services Office
Student Resource Center, C. B. Powell Building
525 Bryant Street, NW
Washington, DC 20059
Phone: 202-806-7513
Fax: 202-462-4267
www.howard.edu/careerservices/
E-mail: careersrhu@howard.edu

Southeastern University
501 I Street, SW

Washington, DC 20024
Phone: 202-488-8162
Fax: 202-488-8093
www.seu.edu

Strayer University—Washington, D.C., Campus
1025 15th Street, NW
Washington, DC 20005
Phone: 202-408-2419, 202-408-2430
Fax: 202-289-1831
www.strayer.edu

Trinity College—Career Services
125 Michigan Avenue, NE
Washington, DC 20017
Phone: 202-884-9636
Fax: 202-884-9241
www.trinitydc.edu/current/career/index.html

University of the District of Columbia
Office of the Vice President for Student Affairs
4200 Connecticut Avenue, NW, Bldg. 39
Washington, DC 20008
Phone: 202-274-5210
Fax: 202-274-6180

Suburban Maryland

CareerNet is the State of Maryland's electronic career and employment information network. CareerNet is part of the one-stop career center concept, which provides several career services in one location. If you need access to the Internet to use CareerNet services, use the public library or the state's employment centers. A list of locations for the centers is listed in this section.

State and County Employment Services—General:

Columbia One Stop
Columbia Job Service/Training Office—Howard County

Oakland Business Center
7060 Oakland Mills Road
Columbia, MD 21046
Phone: 410-312-5760
Fax: 410-312-5761
www.dllr.state.md.us/county/howard
E-mail: columbia@careernet.state.md.us

Frederick County Business and Employment Center (training)
5340 Spectrum Drive
Frederick, MD 21703
Phone: 301-846-2255
Fax: 301-631-2390
www.co.frederick.md.us/jta
E-mail: jta@fredco-md.net

Maryland Job Service (job opportunities)
5340 Spectrum Drive
Frederick, MD 21703
Phone: 301-694-2180
Fax: 301-694-1916
www.careernet.state.md.us/county/frederick.htm
E-mail: onestop@frederick.edu

DLLR—Maryland Job Service
Anne Arundel County Job Service Office
7500 Ritchie Highway, Suite 307
Glen Burnie, MD 21061
Phone: 443-572-0352
Fax: 410-508-2333
www.careernet.state.md.us/county/annearund.htm
E-mail: frickjs@careernet.state.md.us

DLLR—Maryland Job Service
Anne Arundel County Job Service Office
877 Baltimore/Annapolis Boulevard, Suite 360
Severna Park, MD 21146

Phone: 410-315-8873
Fax: 410-315-9838
www.careernet.state.md.us/county/annearund.htm

Montgomery Works
11160 Veirs Mill Road, 1st Floor
Wheaton, MD 20902
Phone: 301-946-1806
Fax: 301-933-4427
www.montgomeryworks.com

Montgomery Works
Lakeforest Mall
701 Russell Avenue
Gaithersburg, MD 20877
Phone: 301-519-8253
Fax: 301-519-8259
www.montgomeryworks.com
(Montgomery Works is Montgomery County's one-stop career services
concept that includes public and private agencies, businesses, and com-
munity organizations.)

Prince George's Workforce Services Corporation
Maryland Job Service Career Net One Stop Center
Washington Homes, 2nd and 4th Floors
1802 Brightseat Road
Landover, MD 20785
Phone: 301-386-5522, ext. 423, 301-386-0701
Fax: 301-386-5533
www.dllr.state.md.us/county/pg/
E-mail: landover@dllr.state.md.us

State of Maryland Department of Labor, Licensing,
and Regulations, Waldorf
175 Post Office Road
Waldorf, MD 20602
Phone: 301-645-8712
Fax: 301-645-8713
careernet.state.md.us/county/charles.htm

Wheaton Job Service—Montgomery County
11160 Veirs Mill Road, 2nd Floor
South Office Building, Suite 100
Wheaton, MD 20902
Phone: 301-929-4350
Fax: 301-929-4383
careernet.state.md.us/county.montgomery.htm

Senior Employment and/or Career Services:

www.mdoa.state.md.us./network/AAAlist.html

Anne Arundel County Area Agency on Aging
2666 Riva Road, Suite 400
Annapolis, MD 21401
Phone: 410-222-4464
Fax: 410-222-4360
www.AA-aging.org

Frederick County Department of Aging
Area Agency on Aging
520 N. Market Street
Frederick, MD 21701
Phone: 301-694-1605
Fax: 301-631-3554
www.co.frederick.md.us/coa

Howard County Office on Aging
Area Agency on Aging
6751 Columbia Gateway Drive, 2nd Floor
Columbia, MD 21046
Phone: 410-313-6410
Fax: 410-313-6540
www.co.ho.md.us/oa/cs_OfficeAging.htm

Montgomery County Area Agency on Aging
Division of Aging and Disability Services
401 Hungerford Drive, 4th Floor
Rockville, MD 20850

Phone: 240-777-3000
Fax: 240-777-1436
www.montgomerycountymd.gov
    click Government on tool bar
    click Aging and Disablility Services

Over 60 Counseling & Employment Service
4700 Norwood Drive
Chevy Chase, MD 20815
Phone: 301-652-8072
Fax: 301-652-8076
www.oversixty.org

Prince George's County Aging Services Division
5012 Rhode Island Avenue
Hyattsville, MD 20781
Phone: 301-699-2696
Fax: 301-699-2857
www.co.pg.md.us
    click Forms and Services
    click A—Find Aging Services

Senior Aides Employment Program
11820 Parklawn Drive, Suite 200
Rockville MD 20852
Phone: 301-255-4206
Fax: 301-231-9360
TDD: 301-881-5263
www.jcagw.org

SeniorNet/JCA at Asbury Methodist Village
301 Russell Avenue
Gaithersburg, MD 20877
Phone: 301-255-4217 (coordinator)
www.seniornet.org/usa/gaithersburg

Senior Service America
8403 Colesville Road, #1200

Silver Spring, MD 20910
Phone: 301-578-8900
Fax: 301-578-8859
www.seniorserviceamerica.org

Specialized Centers—Government and Community Agencies:

Commission for Women Career and Counseling Center
401 N. Washington Street, Suite 100
Rockville, MD 20850
Phone: 240-777-8300
Fax: 301-279-1318
www.montgomerycountymd.gov/cfw
cfw@montgomerycountymd.gov

Foreign-Born Information and Referral Network (FIRN)
5999 Harper's Farm Road
Columbia, MD 21044
Phone: 410-992-1923
Fax: 410-730-0113
firnonline.org
(FIRN serves residents of Howard County for jobs and housing. However, FIRN assists all immigrants with translation and immigration issues.)

Jewish Vocational Services (JVS)
9900 Georgia Avenue
Silver Spring, MD 20902
Phone: 301-587-9666
Fax: 301-587-1541
www.jssa.org/jvs
E-mail: jvs@jssa.org
(JVS serves refugees/immigrants, underemployed adults, career changers, women in transition, and others.)

Professional Outplacement Assistance Center (POAC)
7060 Oakland Mills Road
Columbia, MD 21046
Phone: 410-312-5090, press 0 for POAC receptionist
Fax: 410-312-5091

www.dllr.state.md.us/poac/
E-mail: poac@careernet.state.md.us or sgallison@dllr.state.md.us
(POAC serves individuals who are in professional, technical, and managerial occupations. It provides a computer lab with Internet access, publications and resource materials, individualized career guidance, an audiovisual library, and free services such as faxing, copying, and telephone services.)

TransCen, Inc.
451 Hungerford Drive
Rockville, MD 20850
Phone: 301-424-2002, press 0 for receptionist
Fax: 301-251-3762
www.transcen.org
(TransCen operates a career and placement assistance program for people with disabilities as a public-private partnership.)

Colleges and Universities:

Bowie State University
Career, Cooperative Education, and International Services
J. Alexander Wiseman Center, Room 126
14000 Jericho Park Road
Bowie, MD 20715
Phone: 301-860-3825
Fax: 301-860-3824
www.bowiestate.edu/career_svcs.htm

Capitol College
Career Services
11301 Springfield Road
Laurel, MD 20708
Phone: 301-369-2800, ext. 3093
www.capitol-college.edu/resources/career/index.html
E-mail: careers@capitol-college.edu

Columbia Union College
Career Services
Wilkinson Hall, Room 133

7600 Flower Avenue
Takoma Park, MD 20912
Phone: 301-891-4106
Fax: 301-891-4548

Hood College
Career Center
401 Rosemont Avenue
Frederick, MD 21701
Phone: 301-696-3583
Fax: 301-696-3561
www.hood.edu
E-mail: careers@hood.edu

The Johns Hopkins University
The Career and Life Planning Center
School of Professional Studies in Business and Education
6740 Alexander Bell Drive, Suite 150
Columbia, MD 21046
Phone: 410-290-1933, press 0 for receptionist
Fax: 410-872-9061
www.spsbe.jhu.edu/student/student_planning.cfm
E-mail: careerservices@jhu.edu

University of Maryland College Park (UMCP)
Career Center
3100 Hornbake Library, South Wing
College Park, MD 20742
Phone: 301-314-7225, press 4 for receptionist
Fax: 301-314-9114
www.careercenter.umd.edu
E-mail: career-center-help@umail.umd.edu

University System of Maryland (USM)
The Universities at Shady Grove, Student Services
9640 Gudelsky Drive
Rockville, MD 20850
Phone: 301-738-6023

Fax: 301-738-6050
www.shadygrove.umd.edu

University of Maryland University College
Career and Cooperative Education Center
3501 University Boulevard East
Adelphi, MD 20783
Phone: 301-985-7780
Fax: 301-985-7725
www.umuc.edu/careercenter
E-mail: careercenter@info.umuc.edu

Anne Arundel Community College
Counseling, Advising & Retention Services Center
101 College Parkway
Arnold, MD 21012
Phone: 410-777-2307
Fax: 410-777-2494
www.aacc.edu (search Career Center)

Frederick Community College
Counseling & Career Services Department
7932 Opossumtown Pike
Frederick, MD 21702
Phone: 301-846-2471
Fax: 301-846-2599
www.frederick.edu
    click Student Services,
    click Career Center

Howard Community College
Counseling & Career Services
10901 Little Patuxent Parkway
Columbia, MD 21044
Phone: 410-772-4840
Fax: 410-772-4499
www.howardcc.edu/career

Montgomery College—Germantown Campus
Career/Transfer Center
20200 Observation Drive
Germantown, MD 20876
Phone: 301-353-7772
Fax: 301-353-7839
www.montgomerycollege.edu/Departments/studevgt/Center.htm

Montgomery College—Rockville Campus
Student Career & Advising Career/Transfer Center
Counseling and Advising Building, Room 215
51 Mannakee Street
Rockville, MD 20850
Phone: 301-279-5062
Fax: 301-279-5089
www.montgomerycollege.edu/Departments/studevrv/
transfer-center.html

Montgomery College—Takoma Park Campus
Career/Transfer Center
Student Services Building, Room 131
7600 Takoma Avenue
Takoma Park, MD 20912
Phone: 301-650-1479
Fax: 301-650-1591
www.montgomerycollege.edu/Departments/studevtp/career_main.htm

Prince George's Community College
Career Job Services
Marlboro Hall, Room 2102
301 Largo Road
Largo, MD 20772
Phone: 301-322-0109
Fax: 301-336-9343
www.pgcc.edu/students.html
    click careers/job services
E-mail: CAREER_JOB@pg.cc.md.us

Northern Virginia

CareerConnect is the State of Virginia's electronic career and employment information network. CareerConnect is part of the one-stop career center concept, which provides several career services in one location.

If you need access to the Internet to use CareerConnect services, use the public library or one the following government agencies:

- State of Virginia Employment Commission (VEC) centers
- Workforce centers
- Senior Employment Services Centers (for individuals fifty-five and older)

VEC centers and Workforce centers are at many locations throughout Northern Virginia. You have a choice of location and center. After an intake session, either agency will direct you to the appropriate service for your needs.

State and County/City Employment Services—General:

A. J. Ferlazzo Building Employment Resource Center
15941 Donald Curtis Drive, #180
Woodbridge, VA 22191
Phone: 703-792-4347
Fax: 703-792-4303

Alexandria JobLink
2026 Eisenhower Avenue, Suite 140
Alexandria, VA 22314
Phone: 703-838-4316
Fax: 703-548-0483
www.ci.alexandria.va.us/joblink/

Arlington County Employment Center
3033 Wilson Boulevard, Suite 400B
Arlington, VA 22201
Phone: 703-228-1054
Fax: 703-228-1044

TTY: 703-228-1498
www.co.arlington.va.us/dhs/aec

City of Alexandria—VEC Field Office
5520 Cherokee Avenue, Suite 100
Alexandria, VA 22312
Phone: 703-813-1300
Fax: 703-813-1380
www.vec.state.va.us

Employment Resource Center
Pennino Building
12011 Government Center Parkway, Suite 246E
Fairfax, VA 22035
Phone: 703-324-7280
Fax: 703-449-7908

Fairfax County—VEC Field Office
13135 Lee Jackson Highway, Suite 340
Fairfax, VA 22033
Phone: 703-803-0000
Fax: 703-803-0042, 703-803-1127
www.vec.state.va.us
    click Field Offices, then select Fairfax

Falls Church SkillSource Center
6245 Leesburg Pike, Suite 315
Falls Church, VA 22044
Phone: 703-533-5400
Fax: 703-241-8413
www.myskillsource.org/home/job_seekers/

Lake Anne Employment Resource Center
11484 Washington Plaza West, #130
Reston, VA 20190
Phone: 703-787-4974
Fax: 703-787-9232

Loudoun Workforce Resource Center
Shenandoah Building

102 Heritage Way, NE, #200
Leesburg, VA 20176
Phone: 703-777-0150
Fax: 703-777-0350

Prince William County—VEC Field Office
13370 Minnieville Road
Woodbridge, VA 22192
Phone: 703-897-0407
Fax: 703-897-0440
www.vec.state.va.us

South County Job Source Center
8350 Richmond Highway, Suite 327
Alexandria, VA 22309
Phone: 703-704-6286
www.myskillsource.org

Sudley Employment Resource Center
7987 Ashton Avenue, #200
Manassas, VA 20190
Phone: 703-792-4090
Fax: 703-792-4012

Senior Employment and/or Career Services—
Government and Community Agencies:

Alexandria Senior Services
121 N. Asaph Street
Alexandria, VA 22314
Phone: 703-836-4414
Fax: 703-836-1252
www.seniorservicesalex.org
E-mail: seniorservices@alexandria.org

Arlington Area Agency on Aging
3033 Wilson Boulevard, Suite 700B
Arlington, VA 22201
Phone: 703-228-1700

Fax: 703-228-1148
www.co.arlington.va.us/dhs/aging/aaa/

Fairfax Area Agency on Aging
Employment Training Program
12011 Government Center Parkway, Suite 702
Fairfax, VA 22035
Phone: 703-324-5426, 703-324-5411
Fax: 703-449-8689
www.fairfaxcounty.gov/service/aaa
E-mail: fairfax_aaa@fairfaxcounty.gov

Indo-Chinese Community Center
See Newcomer Community Center

Loudoun County Area Agency on Aging
102 Heritage Way, NE, Suite 102
Leesburg, VA 20176
Phone: 703-777-0257
Fax: 703-771-5161
www.co.loudoun.va.us/services/senior.htm
E-mail: pres@loudoun.gov

Newcomer Community Center
(formerly Indo-Chinese Community Center)
Senior Community Services Employment Program
6131 Willston Drive, Room 8
Falls Church, VA 22044
Phone: 703-241-0300
Fax: 703-241-9546
www.newcomerservice.org/
E-mail: newcomer@newcomerservice.org

Prince William Area Agency on Aging
7987 Ashton Avenue, Suite 231
Manassas, VA 20109
Phone: 703-792-6400

Fax: 703-792-4734
www.pwcgov.org

SeniorNet JCA/TRS-Computer Training Center
2100 Westmoreland Street,
Falls Church, VA 22043
Phone: 301-255-4231
www.seniornet.org/usa/fallschurch

SeniorNet/JCA at Springfield Mall
6691A Springfield Mall
Springfield, VA 22150
Phone: 703-725-4115
www.seniornet.org/usa/springfieldva/

Specialized Centers—Government and Community Agencies:

The Women's Center
133 Park Street, NE
Vienna, VA 22180
Phone: 703-281-2657
Fax: 703-242-1454
www.thewomenscenter.org/
(The Women's Center is a nonprofit resource center that provides afford-
able counseling and education to individuals and families. Personal, professional, legal, and financial concerns are addressed through counseling,
support and therapy groups, workshops, education, and referral services.)

College and University Career Centers:

George Mason University
Career Services
SUB 1, Room 348
4400 University Drive
Fairfax, VA 22030
Phone: 703-993-2370, press 0 to request Career Services
Fax: 703-993-2361
http://careers.gmu.edu
E-mail: careerhp@gmu.edu

Marymount University
Ballston Career Center
1000 N. Glebe Road, 2nd Floor (location)
2807 N. Glebe Road, 2nd Floor (mailing address for main campus)
Arlington, VA 22207
Phone: 703-284-5960
Fax: 703-284-5961
www.marymount.edu/ssa/cccs
E-mail: gradcareer.ballston@marymount.edu

Marymount University
Center for Counseling & Career Services
Main Campus Career Center
Gerard Phelan Hall, 3rd Floor
2807 N. Glebe Road
Arlington, VA 22207
Phone: 703-284-1605
Fax: 703-284-3841
www.marymount.edu/ssa/cccs
E-mail: career.services@marymount.edu

Northern Virginia Community College—Alexandria
Counseling and Career Services
3001 N. Beauregard Street
Alexandria, VA 22311
Phone: 703-845-6301
Fax: 703-845-6485
TDD: 703-845-6016
www.nvcc.edu/stuservices/career.htm

Northern Virginia Community College—Annandale
Counseling Center (CG211, Godwin Building)
Career Resource Work Study Placement Center (CM327)
8333 Little River Turnpike
Annandale, VA 22003
Phone: 703-323-3201 (Counseling)
Fax: 703-323-3229 (Counseling)
Phone: 703-323-3144 (Career)
Fax: 703-323-3233 (Career)

TTD: 703-323-3744
www.nvcc.edu/annandale/anstudentservices/counseling/

Northern Virginia Community College—Loudoun
Counseling Services and Career Resource Center, Room LC 253
1000 Harry Flood Byrd Highway
Sterling, VA 20164
Phone: 703-450-2571
Fax: 703-450-2570
TDD: 703-404-7374
www.nvcc.edu/loudoun/studserv/counseling/default.htm

Northern Virginia Community College—Manassas
The Career Center
6901 Sudley Road, Room 110 Howsman Hall
Manassas, VA 20109
Phone: 703-257-6610
Fax: 703-257-6569
TDD: 703-368-3748
www.nvcc.edu/manassas/student/careerserv.htm

Northern Virginia Community College—Woodbridge
Counseling Center, Room 202
15200 Neabsco Mills Road
Woodbridge, VA 22191
Phone: 703-878-5760
Fax: 703-878-5627
TDD: 703-878-5790
www.nvcc.edu/woodbridge/student/counselingctr

Licensing Contact Examples

This section provides the following licensing contacts:

- general contacts
- comparing licensing requirements of various states

- accounting profession
- engineering profession
- health professions
- legal profession

General Licensing Contacts

The agency you must request for licensing is usually the "state licensing board" for your profession or occupation. Begin with the phone numbers below. You will be routed to additional phone numbers leading to your state board. Also check websites.

Note: See later in the chapter for licensing boards related to accounting, engineering, health, and law.

For District of Columbia License:

DC Department of Consumer & Regulatory Affairs
941 N. Capitol Street, NE
Washington, DC 20002
Phone: 202-442-4320
www.dcra.dc.gov
    click Licenses
    click Occupational and Professional Licenses
    click Information on Boards

For State of Maryland License:

Maryland Department of Labor, Licensing, and Regulation (DLLR)
500 N. Calvert Street
Baltimore, MD 21202
Phone: 410-230-6000
Fax: 410-333-6314
www.dllr.state.md.us/license/occprof/index.html

For State of Virginia License:

Virginia Department of Professional and Occupational Regulation
3600 W. Broad Street
Richmond, VA 23230

Phone: 804-367-8500
Fax: 804-367-2475
www.state.va.us/dpor or www.dpor.state.va.us
  click Boards and Regulation

Comparing Licensing Requirements of Various States

To compare licensing requirements for your profession across the United States, check the requirements set by state boards of licensing for the state or states where you want to practice your profession. You may contact each state board individually. Or here are two ways of obtaining web links for multiple state licensing boards:

1. Ask your national professional association (for example, the American Medical Association) whether they have a list of state licensing boards with web links.
2. As mentioned earlier, the board in each state that awards you your license is usually called a state licensing board. State licensing boards for a particular profession usually belong to their own national association. Obtain the name and website of the national association from your public library reference desk. That national association will likely have web links to every state licensing board that is a member of the association.

Here are examples of national associations of state licensing boards:

- Physicians—The Federation of State Medical Boards at www .fsmb.org
- Architects—National Council for Architecture Registration Boards at www.ncarb.org
- Funeral Directors—International Conference of Funeral Service Examining Boards at www.cfseb.org
- Professional Engineers—National Council of Examiners for Engineering and Surveying at www.ncees.org
- Accountants—National Association of State Boards of Accountancy at www.nasba.org

- Nurses—National Council of State Boards of Nursing at www. ncsbn.org
- Pharmacists—National Association of State Boards of Pharmacy at www.nabp.net
- Attorneys—National Conference of Bar Examiners at www. ncbex.org.

Licensing Contacts for Accounting Professionals

In Washington, D.C., Maryland, and Virginia, only certified public accountants (CPAs) need to be licensed. None of these states in the Washington region require licenses for public accounting, registered public accountants, accounting practitioners, or internal auditors. In all states, state licensing is not a requirement for employment in industry or government; however, check whether a particular employer would prefer that you have a CPA license.

Licensing Boards

District of Columbia Licensing Board:

D.C. Department of Consumer & Regulatory Affairs
Board of Accountancy
941 N. Capitol Street, NE
Washington, DC 20002
Phone: 202-442-4461, 202-442-4320
Fax: 202-442-4528
www.dcra.dc.gov
   click Licenses
   click Occupational and Professional Licenses
   click Board of Accountancy

Maryland State Licensing Board:

Division of Occupational & Professional Licensing
500 N. Calvert Street
Baltimore, MD 21202
Phone: 410-230-6258

Fax: 410-333-6314
www.dllr.state.md.us/license/occprof/account.html

Virginia State Licensing Board:

Board of Accountancy
3600 W. Broad Street, Suite 696
Richmond, VA 23230
Phone: 804-367-8505
Fax: 804-367-2174
www.boa.state.va.us

You may also contact the National Association of State Boards of Accountancy; for additional information, call 1-800-CPA-EXAM. For links to state boards throughout the United States, go to www.nasba.org.

Other Contact Information

National Association:

American Institute of Certified Public Accountants (AICPA)
1211 Avenue of the Americas
New York, NY 10036
Phone: 212-596-6200
Fax: 212-596-6213
www.aicpa.org

Credentials Evaluation:

Each state board in the Washington region has specific requirements for who performs the credentials evaluation. Check with the individual state board.

Licensing Exam:

Uniform CPA exam

Licensing Contacts for Engineering Professionals

Note: Not all engineers need to be licensed. In fact, only about 20 percent of all U.S. engineers are licensed. To decide whether you wish to be or need to be licensed for professional reasons, see www.nspe.org, click Licensure, and read articles related to the advantages of becoming a licensed professional engineer (PE).

Licensing Boards

District of Columbia Licensing Board:

D.C. Department of Consumer & Regulatory Affairs
941 N. Capitol Street, NE
Washington, DC 20002
Phone: 202-442-4320, 202-442-4400; request Engineering Board
Fax: 202-442-4528
www.dcra.dc.gov
    click Licenses

Maryland State Licensing Board:

Division of Occupational & Professional Licensing
500 N. Calvert Street
Baltimore, MD 21202
Phone: 410-230-6322
Fax 410-333-0021
www.dllr.state.md.us
E-mail: pe@dllr.state.md.us

Virginia State Licensing Board:

Department of Professional & Occupational Regulation
3600 W. Broad Street
Richmond, VA 23230
Phone: 804-367-8500
Fax: 804-367-2475
TDD: 804-367-9753
www.state.va.us/dpor
    click Boards and Regulations
    click Apelscidla
    click Apelscidla Regulations
    click General Entry Regulations
    click Professional Engineer
or

www.state.va.us/dpor/ape_reg.pdf
E-mail: apelscidla@dpor.state.va.us

Other Contact Information

National Association:

The National Society of Professional Engineers
1420 King Street
Alexandria, VA 22314
Phone: 703-684-2800
Fax: 703-836-4875
www.nspe.org

Credentials Evaluation:

Engineering Credentials Evaluation International
211 E. Lombard Street
Baltimore, MD 21202
Phone: 410-347-7738
Fax: 410-625-2238
www.ecei.org

Licensing Exam, Professional Engineer (PE):

Exam and other information: National Council of Examiners for Engineering and Surveying
www.ncees.org

Licensing Contacts for Health Professionals

Licensing Boards

Note: For some states listed below, the website will provide phone numbers for the specific professional state licensing board.

District of Columbia Licensing Boards:

D.C. Department of Health
Health Professional Licensing Administration
825 N. Capitol Street, NE

Washington, DC 20002
Phone: 202-442-9200—main number for all health boards; ask for your specific board
Fax: 202-442-9431
http://dchealth.dc.gov/index.asp
    click Professional Licensing
    click Professional Licensing Boards

Maryland State Licensing Boards:

Department of Health & Mental Hygiene
4201 Patterson Avenue
Baltimore, MD 21215
Phone: 877-463-3464, press 0, ask for Liz Groninger; she will connect you to your specific board
Fax: 410-358-1610
www.dhmh.state.md.us/business/prolific.htm
    click Health Professional Licensing Boards

Virginia State Licensing Boards:

Department of Health Professions
6603 W. Broad Street, 5th Floor
Richmond, VA 23230
Phone: 804-662-9900
Fax: 804-662-9943
TDD: 804-662-7197
www.dhp.state.va.us
    click Licensing Boards

Other Contact Information—Selected Professions

Dentists:

- National Association:

American Dental Association
211 E. Chicago Avenue
Chicago, IL 60611
Phone: 312-440-2500

Fax: 312-440-2800
www.ada.org

- Credentials Evaluation:

Educational Credential Evaluators, Inc.
PO Box 514070
Milwaukee, WI 53203
Phone: 414-289-3400
Fax: 414-289-3411
www.ece.org
E-mail: eval@ece.org

- Licensing Exam:

National Board Dental Exam

Nurses:

- National Association:

American Nurses Association
600 Maryland Avenue, SW
Washington, DC 20024
Phone: 202-554-4444, 800-274-4ANA (4262)
Fax: 202-651-7001
www.nursingworld.org
    click International Nursing – at More Links

- Credentials Evaluation:

Commission on Graduates of Foreign Nursing Schools
3600 Market Street, Suite 400
Philadelphia, PA 19104
Phone: 215-222-8454
Fax: 215-662-0425
www.cgfns.org
(The commission prescreens foreign nurses who want to practice in the
United States. It evaluates your educational credentials, checks whether
you were licensed in your home country, and checks your English-
language proficiency. The commission administers a pretest that predicts
your ability to pass the U.S. national licensure exam.)

- Licensing Exam:

NCLEX
National Council Licensure Examination-RN
National Council Licensure Examination-PN

Pharmacists:

- National Association:

American Pharmacists Association
2215 Constitution Avenue, NW
Washington, DC 20037
Phone: 202-628-4410
Fax: 202-783-2351
aphanet.org

- Credentials Evaluation:

Foreign Pharmacy Graduate Examination Committee (FPGEC)
700 Busse Highway
Park Ridge, IL 60068
Phone: 847-698-6227
Fax: 847-698-6238
www.nabp.net (National Boards of Pharmacy)
www.nabp.net/faq/faqfpgee.asp—registration and frequently asked
questions for Foreign Pharmacy Graduate Equivalency Exam

- Licensing Exam:

NAPLEX (North American Pharmacists Licensure Examination), *and*
MPJE (Multi-State Pharmacy Jurisprudence Exam) for Maryland and
D.C. Virginia uses a separate jurisprudence exam.

Physicians:

- National Association:

American Medical Association (AMA)
515 N. State Street

Chicago, IL 60610
Phone: 312-464-5000 main number
Fax: 312-464-4184
American International Medical Graduates Section
Phone: 800-621-8335, ext. 5622
www.ama-assn.org/go/imgs

- Credentials Evaluation:

Educational Commission for Foreign Medical Graduates (ECFMG)
3624 Market Street
Philadelphia, PA 19104
Phone: 215-386-5900
Fax: 215-386-9196
www.ecfmg.org

- Licensing Exam:

USMLE (United States Medical Licensing Examination)

Licensing Contacts for Attorneys

Licensing Boards

District of Columbia Licensing Board:

D.C. Court of Appeals
Committee on Admissions
500 Indiana Avenue, NW, Room 4200
Washington, DC 20001
Phone: 202-879-2710
www.dcbar.org
   click For Lawyers
   click Courts
   click Court of Appeals
   click Committee on Admissions
E-mail: coa@dcca.state.dc.us

Maryland State Licensing Board:

State Board of Law Examiners
Robert F. Sweeney District Court Building

251 Rowe Boulevard
Annapolis, MD 21401
Phone: 410-260-1975
www.courts.state.md.us/ble
E-mail: sble@courts.state.md.us

Virginia State Licensing Board:

Virginia Board of Bar Examiners
Shockoe Center
11 S. 12th Street
Richmond, VA 23219
Phone: 804-786-7490
www.vbbe.state.va.us

Other Contact Information

National Association:

American Bar Association
541 N. Fairbanks Court
Chicago, IL 60611
Phone: 800-285-2221
www.abanet.org

Publication: *Comprehensive Guide to Bar Admissions Requirements.*
Request five-page excerpt containing requirements for fifty states: "Chart
X: Foreign Law School Graduates."
Contact: American Bar Association Section on Legal Education & Admission to the Bar, 312-988-5674, or National Conference of Bar Examiners, 608-280-8550; website: http://ncbex.org/pubs/pdf/2003Comp
Guide.pdf; scroll to page 30 within text for chart X.

Bar Associations (voluntary membership):

Bar Association of the District of Columbia
1819 H Street, NW
Washington, DC 20006
Phone: 202-223-6600
Fax: 202-293-3388

www.badc.org
E-mail: info@badc.org.

Maryland State Bar Association
520 W. Fayette Street
Baltimore, MD 21201
Phone: 410-685-7878, 800-492-1964
Fax: 410-685-1016
www.msba.org

Virginia Bar Association
701 East Franklin Street
Richmond, VA 23219
Phone: 804-664-0041
Fax: 804-664-0052
www.vba.org

Licensing Exam:

Bar examination

Exam and Other Information:

National Conference of Bar Examiners
http://www.ncbex.org

Entrepreneurial Help

The following resources represent examples of entrepreneurial help for you in the Washington area. Check your own community for additional resources. This list includes U.S. Small Business Administration Small Business Development Centers, business incubators for start-up or young businesses, specialized business centers, and high-technology councils. Private business consultants are not listed.

Small Business Development Centers

Washington, D.C.:

D.C. SBDC at Anacostia Economic Development Corporation
2021 Martin Luther King Avenue, SE

Washington, DC 20020
Phone: 202-889-5090
Fax: 202-889-5089

D.C. SBDC at Center for Urban Progress
(bilingual—Spanish)
2000 14th Street, NW, Suite 330
Washington, DC 20009
Phone: 202-671-2828
Fax: 202-671-2597

D.C. SBDC at Howard University
2600 Sixth Street, NW, Room 128
Washington, DC 20059
Phone: 202-806-1550
Fax: 202-806-1777

D.C. SBDC at Howard University
D.C. Department of Employment Services Business Resource Center
64 New York Avenue, NE, 3rd floor
Washington, DC 20002
Phone: 202-671-2177
Fax: 202-671-3073

D.C. SBDC at University of the District of Columbia
(School of Business and Public Administration)
4340 Connecticut Avenue, NW, Suite 507B
Washington, DC 20008
Phone: 202-274-7030
Fax: 202-274-7105

Howard University at Environmental Protection Agency
Office of Disadvantaged Business Utilization Outreach Center
1200 Pennsylvania Avenue, NW, Suite 6402
Washington, DC 20460
Phone: 202-564-4584
Fax: 202-501-0189

Maryland:

Maryland SBDC—Capital Region
(Covers Montgomery and Prince George's Counties)
7100 Baltimore Avenue
College Park, MD 20740
Phone: 301-403-0501, 877-787-7232
Fax: 301-403-0505
www.capitalregionsbdc.umd.edu

Maryland SBDC—Southern Region
(Covers Charles, Calvert, and St. Mary's Counties)
8730 Mitchell Road, PO Box 910 (Must include PO box)
La Plata, MD 20646
Phone:301-934-7583
Fax: 301-934-7681
www.sbdchelp.com
(Inquire about SBDC offices in Calvert County at Prince Frederick, and
St. Mary's County at Lexington Park.)

Virginia:

Alexandria Small Business Development Center
801 N. Fairfax Street, Suite 402
Alexandria, VA 22314
Phone: 703-778-1292
Fax: 703-778-1293
www.alexandriasbdc.com

Arlington Small Business Development Center
3401 N. Fairfax Drive
Arlington, VA 22201
Phone: 703-993-8132
Fax: 703-993-8130
www.arlingtonsbdc.org

Lord Fairfax Small Business Development Center
(at Lord Fairfax Community College)
173 Skirmisher Lane, Suite 317

Middletown, VA 22645
Phone: 540-868-7093
Fax: 540-868-7095
www.lfsbdc.org

Lord Fairfax Small Business Development Center at Fauquier
6480 College Street
Warrenton, VA 20187
Phone: 540-351-1595
Fax: 540-351-1597
www.lfsbdc.org

Loudoun County Small Business Development Center
21145 Whitfield Place, Suite 104
Sterling, VA 20165
Phone: 703-430-7222
Fax: 703-430-7258
www.loudounsbdc.org
E-mail: sbdc@loudounsbdc.org

Mason Enterprise Center/Fairfax–Northern Virginia SBDC
4031 University Drive, Suite 200
Fairfax, VA 22030
Phone: 703-277-7700
Fax: 703-277-7722
www.sbdc.org

Rappahannock Region Small Business Development Center
121 University Boulevard
Fredericksburg, VA 22406
Phone: 540-286-8060
Fax: 540-286-8042
www.jmc.mwc.edu/sbdc

Additional Sources of Business Help:

Community Business Partnership
6911 Richmond Highway, Suite 290

Alexandria, VA 22306
Phone: 703-768-1440
Fax: 703-768-0547
www.cbponline.org

Entrepreneurship Center for New Americans (ECNA) (immigrant focus)
Business Development Assistant Group (BDAG)
George Mason University Enterprise Center
3401 North Fairfax Drive, #225
Arlington, VA 22201
Phone: 703-993-8127
Fax: 703-993-8130
www.bdag.org
(BDAG has an immigrant focus. The organization publishes *A Directory of Language Minority Community Organizations.*)

Ethiopian Community Development Council (ECDC) Enterprise Development Group
1038 S. Highland Street
Arlington, VA 22204
Phone: 703-685-0510
Fax: 703-685-4200
www.ecdcinternational.org
E-mail: info@ecdcinternational.org

Fairfax BioAccelerator (incubator)
7001 Loisdale Road
Springfield, VA 22150
Phone: 703-822-2922
Fax: 703-822-2934
www.fairfaxbiotech.biz

Flory Small Business Center, Inc.
(Cooperates with SBA; nonprofit funded with local funds)
10311 Sudley Manor Drive
Manassas, VA 20109
Phone: 703-335-2500
Fax: 703-335-1700

George Mason Procurement Technical Assistance Program
4031 University Drive, Suite 200
Fairfax, VA 22030
Phone: 703-277-7750
Fax: 703-352-8195

GMU Mentor-Protégé Program at George Mason University
4031 University Drive, Room 205
Fairfax, VA 22030
Phone: 703-277-7731
Fax: 703-383-1204
www.masonenterprisecenter.org/mpp

Greater Reston Chamber of Commerce Incubator
1763 Fountain Drive
Reston, VA 20190
Phone: 703-707-9045
Fax: 703-707-9049
www.restonchamber.org
E-mail: restonbiz@restonchamber.org

Incubator America (George Mason University)
2111 Wilson Boulevard, Suite 600
Arlington, VA 22201
Phone: 703-351-5006
Fax: 703-351-9292
www.incubatoramerica.com

Milestone Equity Partners Incubator
6066 Leesburg Pike
Falls Church, VA 22041
Phone: 703-845-8500
Fax: 703-845-8454
www.milestone-ep.com

Techventure Partnership at George Mason University
Fairfax, VA
Phone: 703-993-4220
www.deq.state.va.us/innovtech/busdevt.html

VA's Center for Innovative Technology
2214 Rock Hill Road, Suite 600
Herndon, VA 20170
Phone: 703-689-3000
Fax: 703-689-3041
www.cit.org/offices.asp

Women's Business Center of Northern Virginia
6521 Arlington Boulevard
Falls Church, VA 22042
Phone: 703-534-6220
Fax: 703-534-6223
www.wbcnova.org
E-mail: info@wbcnova.org

High-Technology Councils:

Fauquier Technology Alliance
PO Box 472
Warrenton, VA 20188
www.fauquiertechnology.org
E-mail: chairperson@fauquiertechnology.org

Northern Virginia Technology Council
2214 Rock Hill Road
Herndon, VA 20170
Phone: 703-904-7878
Fax: 703-904-8008
www.nvtc.org

Technology Council of Maryland
9700 Great Seneca Highway
Rockville, MD 20850
Phone: 240-453-6200
Fax: 240-453-6201
www.mdhitech.org

Washington, DC, Technology Council
1401 New York Avenue, NW, Suite 600

Washington, DC 20005
Phone: 202-637-9333
Fax: 202-637-9393
www.dctechcouncil.org

Chambers of Commerce:

Contact your local public library reference desk for contact information.

Chambers of commerce carry the name of your city, town, or county, or may be specialized and regional according to ethnic group or special interest.

Examples: Fairfax Chamber of Commerce, Rockville Chamber of Commerce, Hispanic Chamber of Commerce (check for more than one county), Women Business Owners of Montgomery County

Economic Development Departments:

Contact your local public library reference desk for contact information. Such departments exist for cities, counties, and states.

Chapter Three

Making American Higher Education Work For You

Whether you need a college degree or a certificate or a single course, explore nontraditional learning opportunities, so you can obtain the education you need to resume or redefine your career as soon as possible. Through such methods you can do one or more of the following:

- Speed up the process of getting a degree or certificate.
- Schedule classes that fit into your busy life.
- Reduce the cost of your education.
- Obtain practical work experience.

Before starting a course of study, you will also want to obtain as much credit as possible for knowledge you already have acquired and credit you already have earned. This chapter explains how.

Note: Consult your school's counselor. To tailor your educational path toward your ultimate career goal, schedule an appointment with the counselor at the school of your choice or at more than one school. A knowledgeable college counselor will help you discover and understand the many program options and nontraditional opportunities available at the school of your choice and in the American higher education system. For specific courses in which you may be interested, a school's counselor might know of courses that may not be printed in the course schedule, but might be listed

continued

on the school's Internet site or might be in the planning stages. A knowledgeable counselor will also refer you to savvy contact persons in specific departments, when appropriate. The counselor will advise you on what courses will be acceptable to the next school where you plan to obtain your terminal, professional, or graduate degree.

While this chapter focuses primarily on earning college credit since such courses can lead to an undergraduate or graduate degree or additional credit that may be required to obtain your state license, you do have other options. You may want to consider auditing a credit course. To audit a class, you must request the instructor's and/or the college's permission—permission is not automatically granted. You must fill out official school forms registering you as an audit student for the particular course. Cost of the course may be the same as if you were attending the course for credit. However, you do not receive a final grade for the course. Therefore, you are not obligated to do homework or take tests.

In the United States, noncredit or continuing education courses are also available. Departments that offer such courses are variously called *workforce development, continuing education, professional development,* and *adult education.* Such courses do not lead to a college degree, and usually vary in intensity and complexity. Such courses vary from a few hours to several weeks, but usually do not last as long as an academic semester. Noncredit courses are offered by various types of institutions:

- Adult education divisions of public schools
- Noncredit divisions of community colleges, four-year colleges, and universities
- Proprietary schools
- Private companies

Students take noncredit courses for a variety of reasons:

- Personal interest to keep up with the latest developments in their fields

- Learning a new skill—word processing or mediation, for example
- Certification in very focused nonacademic areas such as computer applications—Novell, Microsoft, Oracle, or Cisco certification
- Enjoyment—creative writing or music appreciation, for example

EDUCATIONAL NEEDS FOR YOUR CAREER

Some careers require a four-year college degree and even a graduate degree, while others do not. Read job announcements and newspaper ads to determine educational requirements. Also, ask college counselors, friends, and people working in the field of your choice about the educational requirements for the job you want.

Examples of jobs or careers with their requirements:

- Degree—doctor, lawyer
- Certification—computer help desk, automotive repair, locksmith
- Skills—salesperson, some entry-level computer jobs

Certification/Skills

Educational requirements for a variety of careers are changing. The medical and health fields have new career options; you can qualify for some of these by taking short training courses that lead to certification by national organizations. Once certified, you may be able to advance in your career through continued education. Some careers, particularly those in the computer field, require short courses or experience for entry-level positions.

Career center counselors at your local community college can help you select a career and can tell you how to get the required certification.

College Degree

Most well-paid careers still require a college degree, a process that usually takes four years of daytime attendance to complete or eight or more years of evening classes. However, before you get discouraged, you should know that most colleges and universities offer a variety of programs to speed up the degree process; such programs are particularly useful to adults.

CREDIT FOR PRIOR LEARNING

Note: When applying for the following programs, be aware that each college has its own policies about the types of nontraditional courses, programs, and exams for which it will give credit. If you are not currently enrolled at a four-year school but plan to transfer to a four-year school, check the nontraditional course-acceptance policy of the college that will grant your final degree.

There are three ways you can receive college credit from a school you are planning to attend—without taking the equivalent college course.

Transferring Credit

If you have earned credits at another U.S. school or in a foreign country, seek to transfer as much credit as possible to your new school. Do not waste time and money reearning these credits. Sometimes credits can be applied to one degree or major, but not to another. Therefore, be flexible about the degree or major you are now seeking. Each college establishes the maximum number of credits it will accept for transfer— each school sets its own policies.

Submit transcripts from all colleges you have attended (including military transcripts) to the admissions office. The college will notify you how many credits it will accept toward the degree you want to earn. Check the school's procedure before ordering past transcripts.

Testing

You may earn college credit based on test scores of national exams or departmental exams you take, instead of attending the course. Consider this alternative if your school does not recognize your transfer credits, or if you have gained college-level knowledge outside the classroom, or if you have personal expertise in an area.

CLEP (College Level Examination Program) and DSST (Dantes Standardized Subject Tests). CLEP exams are sponsored by the College Board. The CLEP program consists of national standardized examinations (such as biology, English composition, French and college algebra) administered by computer for which you can earn from three to twelve college credits per exam. Credits are awarded based on your exam score. CLEP credits are transferable to most colleges—but check on your school's acceptance policy before you take the exam. Cost ranges from $65 to $85 for each exam, depending on the testing site. (Exam cost is $50, plus $10 for certain essays and an administrative fee added by the testing site.) CLEP exams are a great way to save hundreds of dollars in tuition. Write for information and a free copy of *A Guide to the CLEP Examinations.* Your local library or college may have a copy of this booklet. Address: College Board Publications, Box 886, New York, NY 10101; available online at www.collegeboard.com/clep.

DSST are national exams in subjects such as business, physical science, humanities, social sciences, and applied technologies. Designed originally for the U.S. military, DSST exams are now available to civilian students. DSST exams cost $45 to $60 each. The number of credits earned depends on the score you receive on the exam. Available online at www.getcollegecredit.com.

Departmental College Exams (Challenge and Competency Exams). Many colleges and universities have a list of courses with *challenge exams,* which are tests developed by faculty members who teach the specific course being challenged. You "test out" of these courses by taking one exam that covers all of the material taught in the semester-long course. You are awarded credit, if you earn a minimum score set by the college. You are awarded a letter grade for successful completion of the exam. Each college sets its own policy for awarding grades. *Competency exams* are similar exams but with a P/F (pass/fail) grading system.

Work Experience Leading to Credit

You demonstrate you have learned specific college-level material by compiling a portfolio of your relevant experiences. Through the portfolio, you explain how you have gained college-level knowledge outside the classroom. Your portfolio is evaluated by the college for possible course credits instead of requiring you to attend the course. See www.cael.org.

Colleges call this program by many different names, so you should ask a counselor to identify the program that will allow you to *earn college credit for life experience learning.* Colleges specify the number of portfolio credits students are allowed to use toward their degrees. A typical college might allow students to earn up to thirty credits through this program at a community college, and an additional thirty credits at a four-year college/university. Each college/university sets its own policies.

NONTRADITIONAL WAYS TO STUDY
(LEADING TO CERTIFICATION OR A DEGREE)

There are many nontraditional ways you can earn college credit other than sitting in a traditional learning situation—"home-study" courses, TV, the Internet, or attendance at a conference. You can enroll in intensive recareering programs, or register for traditional courses offered at nontraditional times at your workplace. You may even be able to secure an internship for credit in a new job. Or you may earn college credits for taking on a new project at work—*co-op.* Even recreational activities can sometimes be converted to college credit. Each college/university has its own selection of nontraditional programs.

Independent Learning

Students complete the course requirements on their own, interact with their instructor by phone, mail, or e-mail, and come to campus only for exams. These programs allow students to complete course work during the time that is good for them. An instruction packet is sent to students before the term begins that gives information about books, weekly assignments, grading procedures, and exam dates. Some of these classes combine several disciplines (Example: psychology and sociology). These combined classes may be offered for six credits rather than the usual three credits.

Electronic Distance Learning

Television Courses. Individual colleges accept for credit some educational TV programs (not regular TV) that are produced by academic and media professionals for college credit. The student attends class by viewing a specific TV program, reading the textbooks, and going to campus for exams. Costs are usually the same as for other college credit courses.

Online Courses. One of the newest ways to take a course is via computer. As long as they have access to e-mail and have a compatible computer, students can attend class and interact with instructors and other students via home or work computer. More and more colleges are offering their own online credit and noncredit courses. Online colleges and private online providers also offer courses. Certification courses may include information technology (IT) courses that are certified by companies such as Cisco, Novell, and Microsoft. Individuals who earn certifications from Cisco, Novell, and Microsoft are in demand by employers. These online courses are offered in noncredit formats. If you wish to receive credit for the Cisco class you must attend a two- or four-year college. (Prince George's Community College offers Cisco certification training for credit.) Or you may wish to take the online course and then challenge the credit course at a local college. (See Departmental College Exams above.)

Several of the following sites have interactive IT certification courses. The course providers at those sites also offer business, finance, management, and desktop training online. Here are sample noncredit training providers online (*Note:* This listing does not indicate endorsement of the companies or their programs):

www.ed2go.com
www.mindleaders.com/
www.onlineworkshops.com
www.digitalthink.com
www.learn2.com
www.netG.com
www.howtomaster.com

Computer Conference Format/Satellite Transmission. These are traditional lecture courses that students can attend via computer conferencing or satellite equipment used at multiple sites. The instructor presents a class at one site, and the instructor's presentation is simultaneously broadcast live to other locations and viewed on television or a large projection screen by students at distant sites. This format allows students at the distant site to ask questions, be seen by the instructor and classmates at the originating site, and receive an answer in "real time" while viewing the instructor. Old Dominion University has a degree program that is transmitted to each community college in Virginia. Information is available online at www. ODU.edu/home/distance.

Intensive Recareering in Information Technology

There are intensive courses offered over a brief time period that retrain professionals from other fields who are interested in either computer programming or network engineering. Contact your local community college or private technology schools in the region. Requirements for these fairly new programs are still evolving, so check information provided here when you are ready to consider these programs.

Northern Virginia Community College offers TRIP (Technical Retraining Internship Program), a six-month intensive program, which includes a three-month internship with a company or nonprofit organization, in addition to class work. Requirements are an aptitude exam related to your analytical skills and an interview. Total cost is several thousand dollars. Call 703-323-3102.

Montgomery College in Gaithersburg, Maryland, provides Tech-Leap, a six-month program offered in the evening and on Saturdays, with an internship of up to two months. TechLeap requires at least an associate's degree, as well as an aptitude test and interview. Total cost for tuition and fees is several thousand dollars. Call 301-208-3829.

Courses and Programs with Unusual Course Times, Locations, and Formats

These courses are often in the course schedule, but they may be listed separately from traditional classes. For instance, there may be a list of

Saturday or weekend classes or a list of classes at a specific off-campus site.

Late-Starting Courses. Even if you travel in your job, you may find a conveniently scheduled course. It may begin slightly later in the academic semester than other courses or in the second eight weeks of a semester. Or the course might be compressed into just a few weeks with more hours of instruction at each session.

Weekend Courses. Classes offered on weekends are an option for busy people who cannot take courses on weekdays or evening sessions yet want to go to school.

Off-Campus Courses. Colleges often give courses off-campus at locations near large work centers or perhaps even at your worksite, at convenient daytime hours or shortly after the workday ends. Off-campus locations include high schools, corporate facilities, the facilities of other colleges and universities, and even hotels.

Cooperative Education (Co-op). Students are placed in jobs designed to allow them to learn college-level material on the job. Students generally must have earned at least fifteen credits at the college where they are enrolled before registering for co-op study and must have a minimum grade point average. Contact a counselor at your college.

Recreation and Sports Activities. Some colleges allow students to earn college credit by playing on a college sports team. Contact the coach of the college sports team on which you are interested in playing.

The American Council on Education (ACE) certifies the learning requirements for some recreation programs and makes recommendations to colleges on how much credit to award. For instance, scuba diving certification through PADI Diver training courses allows the student to receive up to seven college credits at institutions that accept the ACE recommendation. Contact PADI Headquarters, 30151 Tomas Street, Rancho Santa, CA 92688. Phone: 949-858-7234. Website: www.padi.com/.

Travel-Study Programs. Students may want to take a travel-study credit course. Students pay for their own travel expenses plus college tuition and fees, so the course may be expensive. The advantage of such a course, in addition to being fun, is that students learn through hands-on experiences.

WEBSITES

For links to many schools in the Washington region, go to www.greaterwashington.org/about_region/education/higher_ed.htm.

For a list of U.S. university websites, go to www.clas.ufl.edu/clas/american-universities.html.

For a list of U.S. community college websites, go to http://utexas.edu/world/comcol/state.

The Council for Adult and Experiential Learning (CAEL) website, www.cael.org, includes a list of publications about nontraditional education for adults. See also www.adultstudent.com.

First Steps

- Contact your college counselor. Your counselor is an invaluable guide for courses and resources.
- Explore whether your school offers nontraditional degree programs.
- Find out if the college you chose offers the program you want. This information is listed in the college catalog, schedule of classes, financial aid brochure, and other printed materials distributed by the college. Also, check the Internet and talk to a counselor at your school. (See also appendix D.)
- If you expect to enroll in a community college for the first two years and then complete your work at a four-year institution, decide on the college to which you will transfer for your last two years of study. Take courses at the community college required by the college to which you will transfer; avoid courses for which you will not receive transfer credit—monitor your status frequently with your college counselor.
- Visit the college's career center to explore various careers and the degrees required. See chapter 2, "Discovering Your Career Options."

QUICK REFERENCE

Educational Institutions of Higher Learning

The following list describes the types of higher education institutions in the United States and their most recognizable program features, although such features may be found at other types of institutions. Whatever school you choose, make sure you find out whether the school is accredited through a reputable national or regional accreditation board or association. Accreditation is a very important credential for a school and can have an impact on your possibilities for financial aid from government sources, as well as professional licensing by state agencies to practice your profession. Also check the school's fiscal soundness. A college counselor can give you this information or point you in the best direction to get it.

Colleges/Universities (public and private). Four-year colleges and universities granting graduate and professional degrees generally attract many students who are continuing their studies after high school. However, some schools may have night programs or special programs for older students. Some institutions, such as the University of Maryland University College, are designed for adult students' need for flexible schedules and a variety of class formats. Examples: public institutions — University of Maryland, George Mason University, University of Virginia, University of the District of Columbia; . private institutions — Georgetown University, Hood College, Catholic University.

Note: For eligible degree programs some colleges and universities have formed consortia that allow students to attend classes at member institutions. See www.consortium.org.

Internet Colleges. The concept of degree-granting Internet colleges is new. The *primary* student body of such schools is made up of adults who take their courses over the Internet. For example: University of Phoenix, which also has traditional campuses, has a large group of students who earn their degrees solely through Internet study. Internet

Higher Education
Quick Reference

colleges/universities enroll students from around the United States and the world. Students must have Internet access.

Proprietary Schools. These are private, for-profit institutions. Tuition may be similar to private, nonprofit schools such as Georgetown University and George Washington University. Examples: Strayer University, Capitol College, Lincoln Technical Institute.

Community Colleges. Community colleges offer only associate's degrees (the first two years of college), but credits can often be transferred to four-year colleges or universities. Community colleges also offer noncredit certification programs and individual courses that can lead to licensure or entry-level jobs. Community colleges usually are the least expensive schools, are usually public, and are found in almost every county in the country. Examples: Frederick Community College, Montgomery College, Northern Virginia Community College, Lord Fairfax Community College, Prince George's Community College.

An Educational Institution's Credentials (Colleges and Universities)

Like the professional licensing you receive to practice your profession, colleges and universities also earn credentials. There are two types: approval by a state and accreditation by an accrediting agency. These credentials prove the institution meets minimum standards. The institution is regularly monitored and evaluated on whether it complies with standards it has agreed to meet. This protects you.

State Approval

Check whether an institution has approval to operate in an educational capacity *with the state where you plan to take classes.* If the institution is not listed on the state website, call the state higher education commission phone numbers below to inquire about the school's approval. You may also ask whether (and what kind of) complaints have been received about the institution.

An educational institution must obtain state approval to operate educationally—and the state requires minimum standards. Depending on the particular state and the type of school, this approval may be referred to as licensing, certification, or simply "approval to operate in an educational capacity." Approval is determined separately by each jurisdiction.

Higher Education Commissions:

District of Columbia State Education Office
Education Licensure Commission
441 4th Street, NW, Suite 350 North
Washington, DC 20001
Phone: 202-727-6436
http://seo.dc.gov
http://dcra.dc.gov
    click Information
    click Education Licensing
(Schools are either approved by the Education Licensure Commission or chartered by the Congress of the United States and exempt from local licensure requirements.)

Maryland Higher Education Commission
839 Bestgate Road
Annapolis, MD 21401
Phone: 410-260-4500; 410-767-0100
www.mhec.state.md.us
    click Higher Education—Colleges and Universities in Maryland
    click Importance of Accreditation
(Approved out-of-state schools are not listed; you must call to inquire.)

State Council of Higher Education for Virginia
Virginia Higher Education Commission
101 N. 14th Street
Richmond, VA 23219
Phone: 804-225-2600
www.SCHEV.edu

Accreditation

This section introduces the concept of accreditation and the need for individuals to be concerned. This section is not designed to provide comprehensive information about accreditation.

What It Is, What It Means . . . Why You Need to Know:

Of course, you want to attend a school of higher education that is reputable. Proper accreditation ensures that a school is reputable and operates with acceptable standards of quality. When you attend a properly accredited school, the education you receive is recognized as valid by licensing boards, employers, government agencies, and others.

In the United States, when an institution of higher education is accredited (has accreditation), it means that it meets minimum standards of quality. These standards relate to curriculum, faculty, facilities, and sufficient funding of the institution for it to operate effectively.

You want to know who is evaluating your higher education institution and/or its programs. Institutions and programs are evaluated by accrediting agencies. If the accrediting agency is reputable, then its evaluation is reputable. If a school meets the accrediting agency's criteria, then it is given accreditation.

Who Accredits Schools and Programs:

Accreditation is provided by private accrediting agencies, not the federal government—unlike most countries, where the ministry of education could approve an institution's minimum standards. State agencies approve postsecondary vocational education and nurse education. Accreditation is optional, though most institutions seek this credential as an indication of the quality of education they provide.

Help for You. The U.S. Department of Education does play an important role, although it does not itself accredit educational institutions or programs. It publishes a list of accrediting agencies that it considers reliable to evaluate higher education institutions. The department provides a list of these recognized agencies at www. ed.gov/offices/OPE/accreditation/index.html. This site will also give you more information about the accreditation concept and process.

Types of Accreditation:

There are two types of accreditation. A particular school can be accredited in one or both ways:

- institutional accreditation—for the entire institution
- programmatic accreditation—for a particular program at the institution, such as its law school

For example, Harvard University is accredited by the New England Association of Schools and Colleges, and Harvard Law School is accredited by the American Bar Association.

Here are just a few examples of accrediting agencies:

Accrediting agencies for an entire institution. Southern Association of Colleges and Schools (one of six recognized regional accrediting agencies); American Association of Bible Colleges; Distance Education Training Council (accrediting agency for institutions that provide distance education).

Accrediting agency for a particular program. American Bar Association.

Questions You Need to Ask:

You want to check three things:

Is the institution and/or program you are considering accredited? The admissions office or an admissions counselor can tell you whether a school is accredited—schools are proud of their accreditation. Accreditation is not automatic. Schools apply for accreditation and must prove they meet standards. Schools working toward accreditation may receive "provisional" accreditation. Schools that do not meet minimum standards may lose their accreditation.

Is the accrediting organization listed by the U.S. Department of Education? Knowing that your institution is accredited is only part of the story. You want to check that the agency evaluating your institution is reputable. If the accrediting agency is recognized by the U.S. Department of Education, you can be confident that the agency is reputable. If it is not listed as a recognized agency by the U.S. Department of Education, find out why.

Here is one reason the accrediting agency may not be listed. The U.S. Department of Education does not recognize some accrediting agencies because they are not linked to federal programs (and therefore you cannot obtain federal aid); but the department recognizes that this is not necessarily a reflection on the quality of the accrediting agency to evaluate institutions.

It is your responsibility to look further into why an accrediting agency might not be listed by the U.S. Department of Education. Some accrediting agencies may not be reputable.

Is the accrediting organization recognized by your state licensing board? Check whether the accrediting agency is recognized by state licensing boards where you eventually want to be licensed to practice your profession. You may also ask the board about the particular school you wish to attend. Contact the state licensing boards.

When Schools Come to You . . .

You may be surprised to discover that you have more college and university opportunities than you realized—and they may be near where you live or work.

The Washington region has institutions with main campuses (examples include Georgetown, University of Maryland, George Mason University, and George Washington University). The region also has institutions that bring their programs to the region, even though their main campuses are located elsewhere. Consider the University of Virginia, a renowned public institution that has its main campus in Charlottesville, Virginia, and also offers degrees at the Northern Virginia Higher Education Center in Falls Church.

Even schools whose main campuses are nearby may have other sites in the region. For example, the University of Maryland, located in the Maryland suburbs, has a site in the District of Columbia; George Washington University, whose main campus is in the District of Columbia, has sites in Northern Virginia and Maryland.

Note: As long as the institution is approved to operate in the jurisdiction where the programs are offered; and the institution is accredited and its programs are nationally, regionally, and/or professionally recognized, you will want to attend the site that has the most effective faculty, and the site that best meets your financial, scheduling, and geographic needs.

Programs offered at "come-to-you" higher education sites are likely characterized by four factors:

- The school's instructional site in the Washington area is an extension of the school's main campus and reputation. Therefore, requirements for taking degree programs and individual credit courses are likely to be the same as if you were attending the school's main campus.
- Those who attend "come-to-you" programs are mainly adults.
- Courses may be offered at convenient hours for working adults, such as lunch time, evenings, and weekends.
- To meet local demand, the school offers selected degree programs, rather than all programs the school offers at its main campus. Such degree programs may be practical and career oriented. Such programs could include business and management, technology, engineering,

nursing, and accounting, as well as other programs for which there might be a student demand.

Here are five ways schools come to you with their credit courses and degree programs. These schools are in the resource directory that follows. Note that such sites may change quickly as student demand changes.

Branch Campuses. Branch campuses have administrators, libraries, and other campus amenities similar to the main campus. An example of a school with branch campuses is Johns Hopkins University. Although its main campus is in Baltimore, it has branch campuses in Montgomery County, the District of Columbia, and Northern Virginia.

Higher Education Centers. Higher education centers are campuses that host two or more universities for specific programs they offer away from their main campuses. The universities hope these programs will appeal to local potential students. The University of Virginia (main campus: Charlottesville) and Virginia Tech (main campus: Blacksburg, Virginia) both offer programs at Northern Virginia Higher Education Center. The Universities at Shady Grove in Rockville, Maryland, hosts seven schools.

Four-Year Schools at Community Colleges. Although community colleges grant only two-year degrees, they may host four-year colleges that offer their programs to the local community. Two examples are Old Dominion University (main campus: Norfolk, Virginia) and Bowie State (main campus: Bowie, Maryland).

Old Dominion University has sites at community colleges in Virginia to offer its satellite broadcast degree programs. Bowie State University offers degree programs at the Montgomery College-Rockville location. And here is a partnership: Northern Virginia Community College at its Annandale campus is opening a medical education center in a partnership with Virginia Commonwealth University and George Mason University.

Leased Space. Some colleges and universities lease space in government buildings or commercial buildings to offer their courses. For example, the University of Maryland's Robert H. Smith School of Business (main campus: College Park, Maryland) has a site at the Ronald Reagan International Trade Center in downtown Washington. Catholic University's Department of Engineering has a site at the Crown Plaza Hotel in Crystal City, Virginia.

Workplace Sites. Your workplace may offer credit courses presented by a local community college or four-year school. Such courses are usually not open to the public. Instead, these are regular college courses selected by the human resources department of your company to meet the educational and workforce needs of employees.

Check with your human resources department to see whether this educational opportunity is available at your company site. If you can bring together a group of at least ten to fifteen people with a request that a particular college course be offered at your company's site, some human resource departments may be able to contact a local college to offer the course.

RESOURCE DIRECTORY

Higher Education Institutions

How to Use This List

- Higher education institutions listed are approved to operate educationally by the state-level jurisdiction in which they offer classes; the institutions are accredited and open to the general public. The listing includes institutions at various higher education levels.
- This is not a comprehensive list. Check your local community library for additional higher education sites; or contact the main campus of a school, whether it is local or headquartered out of state, to ask about off-campus sites in your field, such as nursing, technology, engineering, business, management, architecture, and others. Schools that primarily offer divinity-related degrees are not listed.
- Listings may include more than one phone number to make your search easier, faster, and less frustrating.
- When calling schools, be specific about the information you want, so you are not transferred to several offices. For example, request the experiential learning program and explain that "the program allows adult students to earn college credit for life experience." In

Higher Education
Resource Directory

continued

other cases, request credit courses offered via computer rather than the assessment center, credit courses given in the evenings or weekends rather than adult learning. Terms such as *distance learning, extended learning, adult learning, experiential learning,* and *assessment center* may have varying interpretations.

- Course names may be the same at different institutions, but the content may differ. Go on-site; talk with program directors, department chairs, and faculty. Also determine whether the institution's atmosphere and aspirations reflect your needs and goals.
- When you visit the college website, you may want to use a search box, click on index, or go to the admissions information page.
- Higher education centers that host several schools are marked with an asterisk (*). When calling higher education centers that host several schools, ask whether the schools that the center hosts offer graduate or undergraduate programs, short-term technology certificates, and credit or noncredit courses.

Washington, D.C.

American University*
4400 Massachusetts Avenue, NW
Washington, DC 20016
Phone: 202-885-1000
Fax: 202-885-6014
www.american.edu/

The Catholic University of America*
620 Michigan Avenue, NE
Washington, DC 20064
Phone: 202-319-5000
Fax: 202-319-6171
www.cua.edu/

---

*Chartered by the Congress of the United States and exempt from local (D.C.) licensure requirements and oversight.

118 Chapter Three

Eastern University
School of Professional Studies
444 N. Capitol Street, NW, Suite 422
Washington, DC 20001
Phone: 202-220-1370
Fax: 610-341-1468
www.eastern.edu/professional

Gallaudet University (for deaf and hearing impaired)*
800 Florida Avenue, NE
Washington, DC 20002
TTY/V: 202-651-5000
www.gallaudet.edu/

The George Washington University*
2121 I Street, NW
Washington, DC 20052
Phone: 202-994-4949, 800-447-3765
www.gwu.edu/

The George Washington University
Mount Vernon College
2100 Foxhall Road, NW
Washington, DC 20007
Phone: 202-242-6600
www.mvc.gwu.edu

Georgetown University
37th and O Streets, NW
Washington, DC 20057
Phone: 202-687-0100
www.georgetown.edu/

Howard University*
2400 Sixth Street, NW
Washington, DC 20059

*Chartered by the Congress of the United States and exempt from local(DC) licensure requirements and oversight.

Phone: 202-806-6100
www.howard.edu/

Johns Hopkins University
Arts and Sciences/Advanced Academic Programs in D.C.
1717 Massachusetts Avenue, NW
Washington, DC 20036
Phone: 202-452-1280
Fax: 202-452-8713
www.jhu.edu/advanced

Johns Hopkins University
School of Advanced International Studies
1740 Massachusetts Avenue, NW
Washington, DC 20036
Phone: 202-663-5600
Fax: 202-663-5656
http://sais-jhu.edu

National-Louis University (evenings)
1325 G Street, NW, Suite 740
Washington, DC 20005
Phone: 202-783-1658, 703-749-3000
Fax: 202-638-0199
www.nl.edu

Nyack College, D.C. Campus
Hall of States Building
444 N. Capitol Street, NW, Suite 706
Washington, DC 20001
Phone: 202-220-1300
Fax: 202-220-1305
www.nyackcollege.edu/dc.php

Potomac College
4000 Chesapeake Street, NW

---

*Chartered by the Congress of the United States and exempt from local(DC) licensure requirements and oversight.

Washington, DC 20016
Phone: 202-686-0876
Fax 202-686-0818
E-mail: info@potomac.edu
www.potomac.edu

Smithsonian Associates
1100 Jefferson Drive, SW
Ripley Center 3077
Washington, DC 20560
Phone: 202-786-3228
Fax: 202-357-3715
www.smithsonianassociates.org/masters or
http://ndm.si.edu/EDUCATION/masters.html
E-mail: DecArts@sa.si.edu
(Smithsonian Associates partners with the Parson School of Design, for
a Masters program in the History of Decorative Arts. Parsons School of
Design is a division of New School University.)

Southeastern University*
501 I Street, SW
Washington, DC 20024
Phone: 202-488-8162
Fax: 202-488-8093
www.seu.edu

Strayer University—Washington, D.C., Campus
1025 15th Street, NW
Washington, DC 20005
Phone: 202-408-2400
Fax: 202-289-1831
www.strayer.edu
E-mail: Washington@strayer.edu

Strayer University—Takoma Park Campus
6830 Laurel Street, NW

*Chartered by the Congress of the United States and exempt from local(DC) licensure
requirements and oversight.

Washington, DC 20012
Phone: 202-722-8100, 888-Strayer
Fax: 202-722-8108
www.strayer.edu
E-mail: takomapark@strayer.edu

Trinity College*
125 Michigan Avenue, NE
Washington, DC 20017
Phone: 202-884-9000
Fax: 202-884-9229
www.trinitydc.edu/

University of the District of Columbia*
4200 Connecticut Avenue, NW
Washington, DC 20008
Phone: 202-274-5000, 202-274-6100
Fax: 202-686-0818
www.udc.edu/

University of Maryland, Robert H. Smith School of Business
Ronald Reagan International Trade Center
1300 Pennsylvania Avenue, NW
Washington, DC 20004
Phone: 301-405-5729
www.rhsmith.umd.edu/part mba
    click Evening or Weekend MBA Programs
    click Location

Suburban Maryland

Anne Arundel Community College
101 College Parkway
Arnold, MD 21012
Phone: 410-647-7100

---

*Chartered by the Congress of the United States and exempt from local(DC) licensure requirements and oversight.

Fax: 410-777-2827
www.aacc.edu

Bowie State University
14000 Jericho Park Road
Bowie, MD 20715
Phone: 301-860-4000
www.bowiestate.edu

Capitol College
11301 Springfield Road
Laurel, MD 20708
Phone: 301-369-2800, 800-950-1992
www.capitol-college.edu/

Columbia Union College
7600 Flower Avenue
Takoma Park, MD 20912
Phone: 301-891-4080, 800-835-4212
Fax: 301-891-4023
www.cuc.edu/

Columbia Union College—Gaithersburg Center
201 Perry Parkway, Suite 2
Gaithersburg, MD 20877
Phone: 301-947-7843, 877-246-2225
Fax: 301-987-0563
www.cuc.edu/aep

Frederick Community College
7932 Opossumtown Pike
Frederick, MD 21702
Phone: 301-846-2400
TDD: 301-846-2625
www.frederick.edu

Frostburg State University Center at Frederick
Westview Office Court
5300 Westview Drive

Frederick, MD 21703
Phone: 301-695-3965
Fax: 301-791-4025
www.frostburg.edu
   click FSU Centers

Frostburg State University at Hagerstown
20 Public Square
Hagerstown, MD 21740
Phone: 301-791-4020
Fax: 301-791-4025
www.frostburg.edu
   click FSU Centers

Higher Education & Applied Technology Center (HEAT)*
1201 Technology Drive
Aberdeen, MD 21001
Phone: 410-638-2500
Fax: 410-638-2509
www.heatcentermaryland.com
E-mail: info@heatcentermaryland.com

Hood College
401 Rosemont Avenue
Frederick, MD 21701
Phone: 301-696-3131
www.hood.edu/

Howard Community College
10901 Little Patuxent Parkway
Columbia, MD 21044
Phone: 410-772-4856, 410-772-4800
TDD: 410-772-4822
Fax: 410-772-4803 (specify department)
www.howardcc.edu/
See also Laurel College Center

The Johns Hopkins University
Columbia Center
Columbia Gateway Park

6740 Alexander Bell Drive
Columbia, MD 21046
Phone: 410-290-1777, 301-621-3377
Fax: 410-290-0007
www.jhu.edu
E-mail: colspsbe@jhu.edu

The Johns Hopkins University
Montgomery County Center
9601 Medical Center Drive
Rockville, MD 20850
Phone: 301-294-7000
Fax: 301-294-7010
www.jhu.edu

Keller Graduate School of Management of DeVry University
4550 Montgomery Avenue, Suite 100 North
Bethesda, MD 20814
Phone: 301-652-8477
Fax: 301-652-8577
www.keller.edu/loc_dc_bethesda.html

Laurel College Center*
312 Marshall Avenue
Laurel, MD 20707
Phone: 410-772-4162, 866-228-6110
Fax: 410-772-4161
TDD: 410-772-4171
www.laurelcollegecenter.org

Loyola College, Graduate Center
Columbia Campus
8890 McGaw Road
Columbia, MD 21045
Phone: 410-617-7600
Fax: 410-617-7643
www.loyola.edu

---

*Chartered by the Congress of the United States and exempt from local(DC) licensure
requirements and oversight.

Montgomery College—Germantown Campus
20200 Observation Drive
Germantown, MD 20876
Phone: 301-353-7700
www.montgomerycollege.edu (search Germantown)

Montgomery College—Rockville Campus
51 Mannakee Street
Rockville, MD 20850
Phone: 301-279-5000
www.montgomerycollege.edu (search Rockville)

Montgomery College—Takoma Park Campus
7600 Takoma Avenue
Takoma Park, MD 20912
Phone: 301-650-1300
www.montgomerycollege.edu (search Takoma Park)

Mount Saint Mary's College
Division of Continuing Studies
5350 Spectrum Drive
Frederick, MD 21703
Phone: 301-682-8315, 877-982-2329
Fax: 301-682-5247
www.msmary.edu

Prince George's Community College
301 Largo Road
Largo, MD 20774
Phone: 301-336-6000, 301-322-0866
www.pgcc.edu/
See also Laurel College Center

Southern Maryland Higher Education Center*
44219 Airport Road
California, MD 20619
Phone: 301-737-2500
Fax: 301-737-2542

---

*Chartered by the Congress of the United States and exempt from local(DC) licensure requirements and oversight.

www.smhec.org
E-mail: admin@smhec.org

Strayer University—Anne Arundel Campus
1111 Benfield Boulevard, Suite 100
Millersville, MD 21108
Phone: 410-923-4500 or 877-923-4500
Fax: 410-923-4570
www.strayer.edu
E-mail: annearundel@strayer.edu

Strayer University—Montgomery Campus
20030 Century Boulevard, Suite 300
Germantown, MD 20874
Phone: 301-540-8066, 877-540-8066
Fax: 301-540-8126
www.strayer.edu
E-mail: Montgomery@strayer.edu

Strayer University—Owings Mills Campus
500 Redland Court, Suite 100
Owings Mills, MD 21117
Phone: 443-394-3339
Fax: 443-394-3394
www.strayer.edu
E-mail: owingsmills@strayer.edu

Strayer University—Prince George's Campus
4710 Auth Place, 1st Floor
Suitland, MD 20746
Phone: 301-423-3600, 877-423-3600
Fax: 301-423-3999
www.strayer.edu
E-mail: princegeorges@strayer.edu

TESST College of Technology—Beltsville (AA in Applied Science)
4600 Powder Mill Road
Beltsville, MD 20705

Phone: 301-937-8448
Fax: 301-937-5327
www.tesst.com

University of Maryland, College Park
College Park, MD 20742
Phone: 301-405-1000
www.umd.edu

University of Maryland University College
3501 University Boulevard East
Adelphi, MD 20783
Phone: 301-985-7000, 800-888-UMUC
Fax: 301-985-7978
www.umuc.edu

University of Phoenix
Aberdeen Learning Center
1201 Technology Drive
Aberdeen, MD 21001
Phone: 410-638-2500
Fax: 410-638-2509
www.phoenix.edu

University of Phoenix
Columbia Campus
8830 Stanford Boulevard, Suite 100
Columbia, MD 21045
Phone: 410-872-9001
www.phoenix.edu

University of Phoenix
Rockville Learning Center
9601 Blackwell Road, Suite 100
Rockville, MD 20850
Phone: 240-314-0511
www.phoenix.edu

University of Phoenix
Timonium Learning Center
Timonium Two
1954 Greenspring Drive, Suite 100
Timonium, MD 21093
Phone: 410-560-0055
www.phoenix.edu

University System of Maryland
The Universities at Shady Grove*
9630 Gudelsky Drive
Rockville, MD 20850
Phone: 301-738-6023
Fax: 301-738-6070
www.shadygrove.umd.edu
E-mail: shadygrove@umail.umd.edu

Northern Virginia

Argosy University
1550 Wilson Boulevard, Suite 600
Arlington, VA 22209
Phone: 703-526-5800, 866-703-2777
Fax: 703-243-8973
www.argosyu.edu

Averett University
1593 Spring Hill Road, Suite 100
Vienna, VA 22182
Phone: 703-893-0663, 800-849-9223
Fax: 703-893-7943
www.averett.edu/gps

The Catholic University of America—Department of Engineering
(off-campus site)

---

*Chartered by the Congress of the United States and exempt from local(DC) licensure
requirements and oversight.

Crown Plaza Hotel
1489 Jefferson Davis Highway
Crystal City, VA
(mailing address)
Pangborn Hall
620 Michigan Ave, NE
Washington, DC 20064
Phone: 202-319-5191
Fax: 202-319-4499
http://engineering.cua.edu/engrmgmt/
E-mail: leonardj@cua.edu

Central Michigan University (public university)
5870 Trinity Parkway, #120
Centreville, VA 20120
Phone: 877-679-1268, 703-988-0100 ext. 101
Fax: 703-988-0019
www.cel.mich.edu/locations/default.html
E-mail: centreville.center@cmich.edu

DeVry University—Crystal City (undergraduate)
2341 Jefferson Davis Highway
Arlington, VA 22202
Phone: 866-338-7932, 703-414-4000
Fax: 703-414-4180
www.crys.devry.edu/

ECPI College of Technology
Northern Virginia—Dulles
21010 Dulles Town Circle
Dulles, VA 20166
Phone: 703-421-9191
Fax: 703-674-2144
www.ecpi.edu

ECPI College of Technology
Northern Virginia—Manassas

10021 Balls Ford Road
Manassas, VA 20109
Phone: 703-330-5300
Fax: 703-369-0530
www.ecpi.edu

Florida Institute of Technology Graduate Center
National Capital Region
4875 Eisenhower Avenue, Suite 200
Alexandria, VA 22304
Phone: 703-751-1060
Fax: 703-751-4592
http://ncr.fit.edu
E-mail: flncr@aol.com

George Mason University—Main Campus
4400 University Drive
Fairfax, VA 22030
Phone: 703-993-1000
TDD: 703-993-1002
www.gmu.edu/

George Mason University
Arlington Campus (graduate only)
3401 North Fairfax Drive
Arlington, VA 22201
Phone: 703-993-8999
Fax: 703-993-8995
www.gmu.edu/arlington
E-mail: arlinfo@gmu.edu

George Mason University
Prince William Campus
10900 University Boulevard
Manassas, VA 20110
Phone: 703-993-8350
Fax: 703-993-8418
Princewilliam.gmu.edu or www.gmu.edu

The George Washington University—The Virginia Campus
20101 Academic Way
Ashburn, VA 20147
Phone: 703-726-8200
Fax: 703-726-8248
www.gwvirginia.gwu.edu

The George Washington University—Alexandria
1775B Duke Street
Alexandria, VA 22314
Phone: 703-299-0297
Fax: 703-299-0295
www.gwu.edu/~mastergw/locations/alexandria.html or
www.ocp.gwu.edu

Germanna Community College
Fredericksburg Campus
10000 Germanna Point Drive
Fredericksburg, VA 22408
Phone: 540-710-2000
Fax: 540-710-2101
www.gcc.vccs.edu

Germanna Community College
Locust Grove Campus
2130 Germanna Highway
Locust Grove, VA 22508
Phone: 540-727-3000
Fax: 540-727-3207
www.gcc.vccs.edu

ITT Technical Institute
14420 Albermarle Point Place, Suite 100
Chantilly, VA 20151
Phone: 703-263-2541, 888-895-8324
Fax: 703-263-0846
www.ITT-Tech.edu

ITT Technical Institute
7300 Boston Boulevard
Springfield, VA 22153
Phone: 703-440-9535, 866-817-8324
Fax: 703-440-9561
www.ITT-Tech.edu

James Monroe Center for Graduate and Professional Education
Mary Washington College
121 University Boulevard
Fredericksburg, VA 22406
Phone: 888-692-4968, 540-286-8000
Fax: 540-286-8005
www.jmc.mwc.edu
E-mail: cgps@jmc.mwc.edu

Keller Graduate School of Management of DeVry University
Crystal Gateway Three
1215 Jefferson Davis Highway
Arlington, VA 22202
Phone: 703-415-0600
Fax: 703-415-0700
www.keller.edu/loc_dc_crystal_city.html

Keller Graduate School of Management of DeVry University
1751 Pinnacle Drive, Suite 250
McLean, VA 22102
Phone: 703-556-9669
Fax: 703-556-9420
www.keller.edu/loc_dc_tysons.html

Lord Fairfax Community College
6480 College Street
Warrenton, VA 20187
Phone: 540-351-1505
Fax: 540-351-1540
www.lf.vccs.edu
E-mail: admissions@lf.vccs.edu

Lord Fairfax Community College
Middletown Campus
173 Skirmisher Lane
Middletown, VA 22645
Phone: 540-868-7000
Fax: 540-868-7005
www.lf.vccs.edu

Marymount University
2807 North Glebe Road
Arlington, VA 22207
Phone: 703-522-5600
www.marymount.edu/

National-Louis University
Warren Building
8000 Westpark Drive, Suite 125
McLean, VA 22102
Phone: 703-749-3000
Fax: 703-749-3024
www.nl.edu/

Northern Virginia Community College—Alexandria
3001 N. Beauregard Street
Alexandria, VA 22311
Phone: 703-845-6200
TDD: 703-845-6016
www.nvcc.edu/alexandria/

Northern Virginia Community College—Annandale Campus
8333 Little River Turnpike
Annandale, VA 22003
Phone: 703-323-3000
Fax: 703-323-2163
www.nvcc.edu/annandale

Northern Virginia Community College—Loudoun
1000 Harry Flood Byrd Highway
Sterling, VA 20164

Phone: 703-450-2500
Fax: 703-450-2536
www.nvcc.edu/loudoun/

Northern Virginia Community College—Manassas
6901 Sudley Road
Manassas, VA 20109
Phone: 703-257-6600
TDD: 703-368-3748
www.nvcc.edu/manassas/

Northern Virginia Community College—Woodbridge
15200 Neabsco Mills Road
Woodbridge, VA 22191
Phone: 703-878-5700
Fax: 703-670-8433
TDD: 703-878-5790
www.nvcc.edu/woodbridge/

Northern Virginia Community College Medical Center (scheduled to open Fall 2003)*
Northern Virginia Community College
(in collaboration with George Mason University & Virginia Commonwealth University)
6699 Springfield Center Drive
Springfield, VA 22150
Phone: 703-323-3404
Fax: 703-323-3559
www.nvcc.edu/medical/

Northern Virginia Higher Education Center*
7054 Haycock Road
Falls Church, VA 22043
    Virginia Tech University
    Phone: 703-538-8310
    Fax: 703-538-8320
    www.nvc.vt.edu

---

*Chartered by the Congress of the United States and exempt from local(DC) licensure requirements and oversight.

University of Virginia
Phone: 703-536-1100
Fax: 703-536-1111
www.scps.virginia.edu/northern

Old Dominion University TELETECHNET Locations at community colleges
www.odu.edu
  click Distance Learning Icon
  click TELETECHNET

ODU at Germanna Community College
2130 Germanna Highway
Locust Grove, VA 22508
Phone: 540-423-9117
Fax: 540-423-9214
E-mail: ttngcc@odu.edu

ODU at Lord Fairfax Community College
173 Skirmisher Lane
Middletown, VA 22645
Phone: 540-869-2948
Fax: 540-869-9561
E-mail: ttnlfcc@odu.edu

ODU at Lord Fairfax Community College
6480 College Street
Warrenton, VA 20187
Phone: 540-351-1572
Fax: 540-351-1573
E-mail: ttnlfcc@odu.edu

ODU at Northern Virginia Community College—Annandale Campus
8333 Little River Turnpike
Annandale, VA 22003
Phone: 703-323-3769
Fax: 703-323-3835

Old Dominion University Northern Virginia Higher Education Center
(campus and satellite broadcasts)
21335 Signal Hill Plaza
Sterling, VA 20164
Phone: 703-948-2750
Fax: 703-948-2762
www.odu.edu/nvc

Patrick Henry Community College
One Patrick Henry Circle
Purcellville, VA 20132
Phone: 540-338-1776
Fax: 540-338-8707
www.phc.edu
E-mail: info@phc.edu

Potomac College
1029 Herndon Parkway
Herndon, VA 20170
Phone: 703-709-5875, 888-686-0876
Fax: 703-709-8972
www.Potomac.edu
E-mail: info@potomac.edu

Regent University Graduate Center
1650 Diagonal Road
Alexandria, VA 22314
Phone: 703-740-1400
Fax: 703-740-1472
www.regent.edu

Shenandoah University—Northern Virginia Campus
908 Trailview Boulevard
Leesburg, VA 20175
Phone: 877-680-8971, 703-777-7414
Fax: 703-777-4685
www.su.edu/nvcampus
E-mail: loudoun@su.edu

Stratford University
7777 Leesburg Pike
Falls Church, VA 22043
Phone: 703-821-8570
Fax: 703-734-5339
www.stratford.edu
E-mail: admissions@stratford.edu

Stratford University
13576 Minnieville Road
Woodbridge, VA 22192
Phone: 703-897-1982
Fax: 703-897-1652
www.stratford.edu

Strayer University—Alexandria Campus
2730 Eisenhower Avenue
Alexandria, VA 22314
Phone: 703-329-9100, 877-436-4700
Fax: 703-329-9602
www.strayer.edu
E-mail: alexandria@strayer.edu

Strayer University—Arlington Campus
2121 15th Street, North
Arlington, VA 22201
Phone: 703-892-5100
Fax: 703-769-2677
www.strayer.edu
E-mail: arlington@strayer.edu

Strayer University—Fredericksburg Campus
4500 Plank Road
Fredericksburg, VA 22407
Phone: 540-785-8800, 800-765-8680
Fax: 540-785-8808
www.strayer.edu
E-mail: fredericksburg@strayer.edu

Strayer University Loudoun Campus
45150 Russell Branch Parkway, Suite 200
Ashburn, VA 20147
Phone: 703-729-8800
Fax: 703-729-8820
www.strayer.edu
E-mail: loudoun@strayer.edu

Strayer University Manassas Campus
9990 Battleview Parkway
Manassas, VA 20109
Phone: 703-330-8400, 888-378-7293
Fax: 703-330-8135
www.strayer.edu
E-mail: manassas@strayer.edu

Strayer University Woodbridge Campus
13385 Minnieville Road
Woodbridge, VA 22192
Phone: 703-878-2800
Fax: 703-878-2993
www.strayer.edu
E-mail: woodbridge@strayer.edu

University of Management and Technology
1925 N. Lynn Street
Arlington, VA 22209
Phone: 703-516-0035
Fax: 703-516-0985
www.umtweb.edu
E-mail: info@umtweb.edu

University of Oklahoma
2301 Jefferson Davis Highway
Buchanan Hall
Arlington, VA 22202
Phone: 703-418-4800

Fax: 703-418-2730
www.goou.edu
E-mail: ouinDC@verizon.net

University of Phoenix
Northern Virginia Campus
11730 Plaza America Drive
Reston, VA 20190
Phone: 703-435-4402
Fax: 703-435-2160
www.phoenix.edu

University of Virginia
See Northern Virginia Higher Education Center

Virginia Commonwealth University—School of Social Work
6295 Edsall Road
Alexandria, VA 22312
Phone: 703-823-4130
Fax: 703-823-4148
www.vcu.edu/slwweb/
    click Northern Virginia Campus

Virginia Tech University
See Northern Virginia Higher Education Center

Schools of Art

Art Institute of Washington
1820 N. Fort Myer Drive
Arlington, VA 22209
Phone: 877-303-3771
Fax: 703-358-9759
www.aiw.artinstitutes.edu
E-mail: www.aiw.artinstitutes.edu/requestinginfo_webmaster.asp

The Corcoran College of Art and Design
Admissions
500 17th Street, NW

Washington, DC 20006
Phone: 202-639-1814
www.corcoran.edu/
E-mail: careerservices@corcoran.org

Maryland College of Art and Design
10500 Georgia Avenue
Silver Spring, MD 20902
Phone: 301-649-4454
Fax: 301-649-2940
www.mcadmd.org

Chapter Four

Exploring Financial Assistance for Your Education

Note: For financial aid information on how to start a business, consult the U.S. Small Business Development Centers listed in chapter 2, "Resource Directory, Entrepreneurial Help."

Choosing the college or university you want to attend may depend on the kind and amount of financial aid you can receive to help pay for tuition and other costs. All colleges and universities do not offer the same types of assistance, so it may be important for you to contact several schools.

General Sources and Types of Financial Aid

Financial assistance can come from several sources: federal, state, institutional (meaning individual college or university funds), and private groups. The type of assistance can be in the form of scholarships, grants, loans, and work-study jobs.

- Grants and scholarships are most often considered "gift" aid and don't have to be repaid.
- Loans are funds that must be paid back to the lender. Loans can be offered at low interest rates, and payments may not begin until the student finishes school. (Where there is a need for specific professions, government sources may cut back on the loan amount to be repaid—for example, teachers in some states.)
- Work-study jobs are college-sponsored jobs, either on or off campus, for which you get paid by the hour. Students must be paid at least the federal minimum wage. There is no maximum wage rate.

Some private organizations—such as churches, chambers of commerce, and business and professional groups—may also help academically promising students with scholarships. In addition, employers may have tuition assistance available as a benefit to their employees. Check with your employer about this possibility.

Large universities that have fellowships and internships may be more likely to have institutional funds that can be awarded to academically gifted students. Contact both local community colleges, and university financial aid offices to explore options that may be available to you.

How Your Financial Need Is Determined. Here is the process used to determine financial need:

1. Information you submit in the Free Application for Federal Student Aid (FAFSA) determines your expected family contribution (EFC) toward your education.
2. Each institution constructs a budget for you that includes its tuition and fees, an allowance for room and board (an estimate based on living on campus, living off campus, or living at home with parents), an allowance for books and supplies, an allowance for personal expenses, and an allowance for transportation to classes.
3. Your EFC is subtracted from this budget to determine your financial need at each institution. The institution then notifies you of your financial aid package. Due to an institution's limited resources, this dollar amount may not meet your financial need. The earlier you apply and complete your file, the more likely resources will be available.

Federal Financial Aid

Financial aid provided by the federal government is the major source of student aid. It is the first source for you to consider. For information, call 1-800-4fedaid.

The Free Application for Federal Student Aid is the basic form used by all postsecondary institutions to determine need for federal aid at both the undergraduate and graduate levels.

Filling out an application for federal financial aid is a good step, even if you do not think you will be eligible. Individual colleges usually use that application to get information about your financial situation.

For a basic understanding of the federal financial aid process, see this chapter's "Quick Reference"section: "Types of Financial Federal Aid" and "Tips for Completing FAFSA." For more detailed information, see *The Student Guide: Financial Aid* from the U.S. Department of Education. It is published annually and is available at your school financial aid office or online at http://studentaid.ed.gov/students/publications/student_guide/index.html. You may also contact the U.S. Department of Education at 1-800-4fedaid.

Other Financial Aid Sources

State Aid

Maryland, Virginia, and the District of Columbia have scholarship programs for their residents. There is a residency requirement to qualify. The awards are based on need and merit. The following websites detail what is available, who is eligible, and how to apply:

- Maryland residents: www.mhec.state.md.us/financialAid/index.asp, Phone: 410-260-4565
- Virginia residents: www.explorevirginiacolleges.com/students/payforcollege.asp
  click Adult Learners
  click Paying for College
  click Financial Aid Links or Academic Common Market
- District of Columbia residents: http://seo.dc.gov/services/post_secondary_financial_assistance/index.shtm, Phone: 202-727-2824 or 202-727-6436

If you plan to attend school outside of the Washington, D.C., metropolitan area, call 800-872-5327 or check www.ed.gov/Programs/bastmp/SHEA.htm for information on all states.

School Aid

Contact (on the phone, in person, or by e-mail) the financial aid office of every school you are interested in attending. Ask about scholarships and financial aid provided by the school, in addition to asking whether the school participates in federal aid programs:

- Do you have any special scholarships that require additional applications, and what are those deadlines? For example, institutions may have funds that are targeted for particular populations, so the institutions need to know more about you to match you with a scholarship. As with most scholarships, there is much competition for these awards.
- Are there other places on campus to contact about sources of aid? For graduate students, there may be a special office as well as the student's subject area departments to learn about fellowship and assistantship opportunities. Some schools may offer aid through the following sources:

  student activities
  athletic department
  alumni office
  departments in your specialty or major
  ethnic campus groups

- Do you have a bulletin board or notebook where you post scholarship opportunities? Colleges and universities often receive notification and applications for special scholarships.
- Does the institution have any special payment plans? Many schools participate in programs that allow you to pay your bill in installments.

Ask about the institution's unique financial aid process:

- What forms are required to apply for aid at your school? Some schools require the College Scholarship Service (CSS) Profile, in addition to the FAFSA. Schools may have their own forms for you to complete. Don't assume that all schools require the same forms. Filling out the wrong forms will delay your application.
- What are the deadlines or priority dates to submit all paperwork? Each school sets deadlines for receiving its required forms. Funds are limited. The sooner you submit your paperwork, the more resources will be available to you. If you file late, your application may not be accepted.

  If you need to send material directly to the school, send it by overnight mail, so that you have the name of who received it. Check with the financial aid office to find out whether an overnight service (such as FedEx or UPS) or U.S. mail is received directly in the financial aid office. Generally, mail via the U.S. Postal Service is received in a mailroom and then delivered to the office.

- When can you expect to hear about your financial aid? Dates vary widely among schools. All schools wait until you are admitted to a degree program. Some schools mail all their award letters on the same day. Others send them out on a rolling basis.
- What is the procedure to notify the institution of any special circumstances that affect your ability to pay for your education? There are many such circumstances. These include unemployment, pay reduction, and high medical costs. You will need to provide documentation for any of these situations. The agency or institution awarding you financial aid may help further, when you are faced with special circumstances.

Occupation-Related Financial Aid—Some Examples

For various occupational groups, you can contact:

Medical School. Application and fees (www.aamc.org/students/start.htm), Phone: 202-828-0600

Nursing Profession. U.S. Department of Health and Human Services (bhpr.hrsa.gov/nursing/loanrefaq.htm), Phone: 866-813-3753; and the National League for Nursing (www.nln.org), click Foundation for Nursing Education; Phone: 800-669-1656

Dental Profession. (www.ada.org/ada/charitable/endow), Phone: 312-440-2567

Pharmacists. (www.aphafoundation.org/scholarship/student_scholarship.htm), Phone: 703-739-2330

Private and Corporate Financial Aid

Many individuals, organizations, and corporations sponsor scholarships. You should contact any organization of which you are a member, such as a religious group, ethnic group, occupational organization, or social club, to see if it sponsors a scholarship.

There are also nonprofit clubs of businesspersons in your local community that provide small financial aid awards or may be able to direct you to sources. The phone numbers for such clubs may be available through your public library. Such clubs include Kiwanis International (kiwanis.org), Women Business Owners of Montgomery County (www.wbo-mc.com), and Rotary International (rotary.org). You may wish to attend a meeting to meet the members.

There are many websites that will assist you in finding these types of scholarships. They will ask you questions about yourself and then do a match against their databases. Since many organizations offer this as a free service, there is no need to pay to have a search done for you. In addition to those listed below, check each college website for links to sources of information they recommend.

www.fastweb.com
www.hsf.net
www.collegeinfo.org
www.finaid.org/finaid.html
www.collegenet.com/about/index_html
www.college-scholarships.com

Alternative Loans

If you are not offered enough financial aid, alternative loans may be available to you. Such loans should be used only as an extreme measure. They are called alternative loans because they are not part of the federal loan programs in which most students participate. They generally have higher interest rates, require a cosigner, and cannot be consolidated with other educational loans you may have. Check with the institution you plan to attend regarding the alternative loans they process. Many have arrangements with specific lenders to offer better terms for that school's students.

The amount you borrow through alternative loan programs may affect your eligibility for other financial aid. All loans need to be repaid or your credit rating will be affected. So all loans not yet repaid are considered when you are seeking other forms of credit such as credit cards, home mortgage, or car loans. You may be denied credit, even on alternative loans, when your debt-to-income ratio is reviewed. There may be employment consequences as many employers do credit checks before hiring.

Aid through Your Creative Search

1. Look for area businesses in your field willing to sponsor promising future employees. In addition, some communities with a shortage of professionals in your field may be willing to help pay for your education, in return for your commitment to work in the community when you have graduated and become licensed, if applicable. This is an entrepreneurial search on your part.

2. If you are eligible for support from social service agencies, use their help to find housing, food programs, and jobs to help with the other aspects of your life.
3. Consider moving from the Washington, D.C., area to a lower cost of living area to pursue your education (see appendix D).
4. Establish residency ("domicile") where the school is located, to qualify for the lowest tuition rates at the public institution of your choice. Determine what residency means for that particular school. For example, state universities or community colleges may look to see that you are registered to vote in their states, that your car is registered there, that you pay rent locally. *Note:* "In-county" tuition is the lowest rate charged by public institutions. Some schools, particularly community colleges, charge "out-of-county" and "out-of-state" tuition. The highest rate charged by public institutions is for out-of-state tuition.
5. Your state might have arrangements with other states to provide education in certain fields at reduced tuition rates. This is sometimes known as the academic common market.

Getting Help to Plan Your Student Financial Aid

If you want help finding sources of financial aid, you have many free sources:

* Financial aid office of the school you may want to attend.
* Websites that ask for information about you and provide financial aid
* Federal and state agencies.
* Associations in your profession that provide loans or endowments to help students. You can explore whether your association provides these opportunities by asking the national association in your profession and checking the list in this chapter under "Occupation-Related Financial Aid."

If you wish to pay a private financial aid consultant or wish to pay for a scholarship search, you may want to ask a friend for the name of a counselor who has been helpful. Please read the information provided by the National Association of Student Financial Aid Administrators at www.nasfaa.org/publications/2000/Consultantsservices. asp.

Websites

In addition to websites provided in this chapter, there are websites that can give you general information about financial aid, as well as advice on finding help with the process:

www.students.gov
www.finaid.org
www.studentaid.ed.gov

First Steps

1. **Complete the FAFSA.** To apply for federal financial aid, you must complete the Free Application for Federal Student Aid (FAFSA). From this application you will receive a Student Aid Report (SAR), which will show your expected family contribution and your eligibility to receive the Federal Pell Grant. The FAFSA will also be used to see whether you qualify for other federal aid.

   Even if you do not think that you will be eligible, filing the FAFSA form is usually helpful. The financial aid office at the school you hope to attend will probably need the Student Aid Report that results from the FAFSA to decide whether to offer you any aid directly from the college.

2. **Search for financial aid sources.** Search in the following order:

   Federal and/or state aid
   School aid and/or professional aid
   Private and corporate aid
   Aid through your creative search

3. **Get help searching.** Use the following resources:

   School financial aid counselor in Financial Aid Office
   Federal and state agencies
   Associations in your profession that provide loans or endowments to help students

QUICK REFERENCE

Federal Financial Aid Opportunities

There are several types of federal financial aid provided by the U.S. Department of Education. Most, not all, schools participate in these financial aid programs. You must check with your individual school to learn what programs it participates in. The amount of funding for each program varies, so not all students who qualify will receive funds.

Note: General information is provided here. Check with your financial aid counselor for further details. See also *The Student Guide: Financial Aid* from the U.S. Department of Education, published annually and available at your financial aid office or online at http://studentaid. ed.gov/students/publications/student_guide/index.html. You may also contact the Department of Education at 1-800-4fedaid.

- Federal Pell Grants—provided for low-income students; as grants, they do not need to be repaid.
- Federal Supplemental Opportunity Grant—additional grant money for Federal Pell Grant recipients.
- Federal Family Loan Program—includes the Federal Subsidized Stafford Loan, the Federal Unsubsidized Stafford Loan, and the Federal Parent Loan for Undergraduate Students (PLUS); interest rates are variable.
- Perkins Loans—low-interest loans made by the institution with government funds.
- Federal work-study programs—on-campus jobs and community service jobs for enrolled students.

General Eligibility Criteria and Restrictions for Federal Educational Financial Aid

Note: General eligibility criteria and restrictions are provided here. Check with your financial aid counselor for further details. See also *The Student Guide: Financial Aid* from the U.S. Department of Education, published annually and available at your financial aid office or online at http://studentaid.ed.gov/students/publications/student_guide/index.html. You may also contact the Department of Education at 1-800-4fedaid.

Criteria for Federal Financial Aid Eligibility

- Must be a U.S. citizen or an eligible noncitizen (see below).
- Must have a high school diploma or equivalent.
- Must be admitted into a degree or a certificate program that qualifies for financial aid. (You may apply before you are admitted. In many cases, you may need to apply before you are admitted so that you know your financial aid package before placing a deposit. Financial aid does not usually cover the admission deposit.)
- Must register with Selective Service, if a male between eighteen and twenty-six years old. This applies to all U. S. citizens and eligible noncitizens.
- Must demonstrate financial need, except for some loan programs (such as Federal Unsubsidized Stafford Loan and various alternative loans).
- Must have a valid social security number.
- Must not owe a refund on a federal student grant or be in default on any federal student loans.
- To remain eligible, a student must make satisfactory academic progress according to the financial aid standards of the college or university.

Immigrants who hold any of the following immigration documents or a "green card" are eligible to apply for federal financial aid, such as Federal Pell Grants, Federal Stafford loans, Federal Perkins Loans, and Federal work-study jobs:

- I-151, I-551, I-151C, or I-688
- I-797 along with approved immigrant visa
- I-94 showing any of the following designations: Refugee, Asylum Granted, Indefinite Parole, Humanitarian Parole, or Cuban-Haitian entrant

Restrictions on Federal Financial Aid

Visas—International Students:

If you are in the United States on an F1 or F2 student visa, or a J1 or J2 exchange visitor visa, or a G series visa, you are not eligible for assistance that is federally funded. These visa types show that you are an international student.

The websites below can help you find information on financial assistance. They give information about the type of assistance, eligibility criteria, and application procedures.

www.internationalstudent.com—the International Student Resource Center offers advice, information, and resources for the international college student.

www.edupass.org—the most complete site for international students on financial assistance and other useful information about college.

www.iefa.org—International Education Financial Aid offers a searchable database of international student scholarships, grants, and awards.

Financial assistance for international students is limited. Persistent and patient research is necessary to locate all possible sources of aid.

Educational Attainment:

All federal loans have borrowing limits based on your school level and previous borrowing.

• Federal Pell Grants—students who already have a bachelor's or professional degree (earned in the United States or abroad) will not be eligible for the Federal Pell Grant, with the exception of some teacher certification programs. Check with the college or university you decide to attend to see if its teacher certification program is eligible for Federal Pell Grants.
• Federal Stafford Loans—the program is available to all qualified students who have not exceeded their borrowing limits. Therefore, you may obtain a loan for a first or second bachelor's degree, if you have not used up your lifetime limit on borrowing Stafford funds toward a bachelor's degree. You may obtain a loan for a master's degree, a doctorate, or a professional degree, if you have not used up your maximum lifetime borrowing limit for graduate degrees.

Availability of Funds:

Federal Supplemental Opportunity Grants, Federal work-study, and Federal Perkins Loans are available to the extent that schools have the funds to offer these awards. Institutions are given limited funds from the federal government for these programs.

Tips for Completing FAFSA (Free Application for Federal Student Aid)

Note: General information is provided here. Check with your financial aid counselor for further details. See also *The Student Guide: Financial Aid* from the U.S. Department of Education, published annually and available at your financial aid office or online at http://studentaid .ed.gov/students/publications/student_guide/index.html. You may also contact the Department of Education at 1-800-4fedaid.

Take the time to complete the application correctly to avoid delays that may jeopardize your financial aid chances. The FAFSA directions are clear, so don't be intimidated by the form's length. You will need copies of your most recent tax return and any current bank statements. A complete list of suggested items can be found at www.fafsa.ed.gov or in the FAFSA booklet. If you have not yet filed your tax return, you may wish to use your year-end pay stub for estimating the information.

Here are some other suggestions to help you with the process:

- For the fastest processing, file FAFSA online at www.fafsa.ed.gov. You may also file a paper FAFSA.
- Get a pin number to sign your FAFSA online at www.pin.ed.gov.
- Answer all questions. Leaving items blank may delay the processing of your aid while each school requests the information from you and then processes the information.
- Be consistent with the spelling of your name. Your admissions record, your immigrant documents, and your social security card should all match. Inconsistencies can delay processing because they must be resolved.
- Make sure you use the correct social security number. The U.S. Department of Education does matches against numerous databases using this number.
- For state aid consideration, provide state information on the FAFSA form.

- Don't forget to include the school codes for all the schools to which you want your information sent. Codes are available from the schools themselves or from FAFSA.
- Don't forget to sign the paper FAFSA, print and sign the signature page if online without a PIN, or sign using a PIN online. If you do not use your PIN, your signature must be mailed to the address provided. Your information will not be processed without your signature.
- Keep a copy of the information you submit, as well as copies of the worksheets.
- Check the accuracy of the Student Aid Report (SAR). The SAR is the feedback sent to you from the U.S. Department of Education containing the FAFSA information you submitted. The SAR is sent to schools where you have requested financial aid. You may have mistyped a number or placed it on the wrong line. You may file a correction online or use the paper SAR that is mailed to you.

Useful Phone Numbers, Agencies, and General Resources

SELECTED LIBRARY REFERENCE SERVICES

Fairfax City Regional Library—703-246-2281, request reference
Alexandria Central Library—703-519-5900, request reference
Arlington County Central Library—703-228-5990, request reference
Montgomery County Library Telephone Reference—240-777-0001

Night Owl Service (telephone reference)—Maryland
800-325-NITE (Maryland 800 number)
weeknights after the local public libraries close—until 11 p.m.

Washington, D.C.—Martin Luther King Library
Washingtoniana Division—202-727-1213 or 202-727-0321 (main library number)
College Information Center (Martin Luther King Library)—202-393-1100

To contact other libraries in the Metropolitan Washington area, check *Passport to Your Local Libraries* (11 public library systems, 137 branches), available online at www.mwcog.org/publications/passport/default.asp.

For academic, government, and other types of libraries, also check www.fairfaxcounty.gov/library/internet/libraries.htm.

TO CHECK ON A PARTICULAR BUSINESS OR FILE A COMPLAINT

Contact the Better Business Bureau (a private organization), or consumer affairs offices (government agencies).

155

Better Business Bureaus

Better Business Bureau of Metropolitan Washington and Eastern Pennsylvania—Phone: 202-393-8000, www.mybbb.org, E-mail: info@dc.bbb.org

Better Business Bureau of Greater Maryland (distant Washington suburbs)—Phone: 410-347-3992, www.baltimore.bbb.org, E-mail: info@bbmd.org

Better Business Bureau of Central Virginia (for distant Washington suburbs)—Phone: 804-648-0016, www.richmond.bbb.org, E-mail: info@richmond.bbb.org

Consumer Affairs Offices

Washington, D.C.

DC Consumer and Regulatory Affairs Department—202-442-4400

Maryland

Montgomery County—240-777-3636
Howard County—410-313-6420
For other counties in Maryland, call the State of Maryland Consumer
   Protection Hotline—410-528-8662

Virginia

Alexandria Office of Consumer Affairs—703-838-4350
Arlington Office of Consumer Affairs—703-228-3260
Fairfax Office of Consumer Affairs—703-222-8435
For other counties, contact the State of Virginia Office of Consumer
   Affairs—804-786-2042
www.vdacs.state.va.us/consumers

TO CHECK ON PARTICULAR SCHOOLS

District of Columbia State Education Office
Education Licensure Commission

441 Fourth Street, NW, Suite 350 North
Washington, DC 20001
Phone: 202-727-6436
http://seo.dc.gov
http://dcra.dc.gov
  click Information
  click Education Licensing
(The District of Columbia Education Licensure Commission's jurisdiction covers schools that hold classes in Washington, D.C.; however, the Commission does not have jurisdiction over Congressionally
chartered schools. For a list of those schools, see the Resource Directory for chapter 3.)

Maryland Higher Education Commission
839 Bestgate Road,
Annapolis, MD 21401
Phone: 410-260-4500, 410-767-0100
www.mhec.state.md.us

State Council of Higher Education for Virginia
Virginia Higher Education Commission
101 N. 14th Street
Richmond, VA 23219
Phone: 804-225-2600
www.SCHEV.edu

GENERAL RESOURCES

Most of these widely used resources are available at your public library
reference desk.
Washington 2003—A Comprehensive Directory. 19th ed. Washington,
  DC: Columbia Books, Inc., 2002. Published annually. Provides
  names and address of institutions, agencies, and companies, with key
  decision makers and contact information. Organized by type of institution: U.S. government, local governments, media, etc.
Congressional Quarterly. *Washington Information Directory
  2003–2004.* Washington, D.C.: CQ Press, 2003. Published annually.

Provides names and address of institutions, agencies, and companies, with key decision makers and contact information. Organized
by subject.
Washington Business Journal. *The Book of Lists: Who's Who and
What's What in Greater Washington Business 2003*. McLean, Va.:
American City Business Publications, Inc., 2003. Published annually. Provides company rankings in a variety of fields, as well as
decision makers with contact information. Available at your public
library reference desk.
Metropolitan Council of Governments. *Strengthening Immigrant Families in the Washington Metropolitan Region: A Directory of Resources*, November 2000. Available free by calling 202-962-3256.
While some contact information may be outdated, you will have an
idea of the resources in the region.

SELECTED U.S. GOVERNMENT
AGENCIES AND PHONE NUMBERS

Bureau of Citizenship and Immigration Services—BCIS (U.S. Department of Homeland Security; formerly Immigration and Naturalization
Service—INS; U.S. Department of Treasury)
Phone: 800-375-5283 (automated; also, select customer service representative option)
www.BCIS.gov
Phone/web: Information about the nearest BCIS office, immigration information, "green card"

U.S. Social Security Administration
Phone: 800-772-1213 (least busy: Wed., Thurs., Fri., 4–7 p.m.)
(automated; also, select customer service representative option)
www.ssa.gov; www.ssa.gov/locator
Phone/web: Use to find the office nearest you and other information

U.S. Department of Labor
Referral and Information Line
Phone: 866-4-USA-DOL

U.S. Department of Labor
Office of Apprenticeship Training, Employer and Labor Services
(OATELS)
200 Constitution Avenue, NW
Washington, DC 20210
Phone: 877-872-5627 for information on Maryland, Virginia, D.C. programs; also 202-693-2796
www.doleta.gov/atels_bat
click State Information, then select a state—website links to state programs

U.S. Department of Labor
Veterans' Employment and Training Service (VETS)
200 Constitution Avenue, NW, Room S-1325
Washington, DC 20210
Phone: 202-693-4700
Fax: 202-693-4754
www.dol.gov/vets

U.S. Department of Labor
Women's Bureau, Room S-3311
200 Constitution Avenue, NW
Washington, DC 20210
Phone: 1-800-827-5335, 202-693-6710
Fax: 202-693-6725
www.dol.gov/dol/wb

U.S. Department of Health and Human Services
Administration for Children and Families
(Refugee Assistance, Administration on Aging, Office of Community Services)
901 D Street, SW
Washington, DC 20447
Toll-free: 877-696-6775
www.acf.hhs.gov/programs.html
Administration for Children and Families:
  Phone: 215-861-4000
  Fax: 215-861-4070

Refugee Resettlement:
  Phone: 202-401-9246
  Fax: 202-401-0981
Office of Community Services:
(grants to state and local governments, community action agencies and
community development corporations)
  Phone: 202-401-9333
  Fax: 202-401-1556

U.S. Department of Education
Office of Vocational and Adult Education
4090 MES
400 Maryland Avenue, SW
Washington, DC 20202
Phone: 202-205-5451
Fax: 202-205-8748
www.ed.gov/offices/OVAE/
E-mail: ovae@ed.gov

ASSOCIATIONS

American Staffing Association
277 S. Washington Street, #200
Alexandria, VA 22314-3646
Phone: 703-253-2020
Fax: 703-253-2053
www.staffingtoday.net

International Association of Counseling Services
101 S. Whiting Street, Suite 211
Alexandria, VA 22304
Phone: 703-823-9840
http://iacsinc.org

The National Board for Certified Counselors
3 Terrace Way, Suite D
Greensboro, NC 27403-3660
Phone: 336-547-0607
www.nbcc.org

Pre-Resume Questionnaire

Here are questions to consider and fill out before seeing a career or college counselor—and before preparing a resume. The background you provide will help others guide you. Your prospective employer may also ask you some of these questions in an interview—and you will have the information ready.

MY BACKGROUND

I have been in the United States since _____.

Currently (check one):
_____ I am a student with a _____ type of visa.
_____ I have a green card.
_____ I became a U.S. citizen on _____.
_____ I will become a U.S. citizen on _____.

I speak the following languages: _____.

My native country is _____.

I last lived in _____.
This is a (check one):
_____ village
_____ town
_____ mid-sized city
_____ large city (how large?_____ people; give the number of people)

Just before coming to the United States, my last job was _____ .

The name of the last place where I worked before coming to the United States is _____ .

Address of that employer is _____ .

Circle one:
(**YES I can** or **NO I cannot**) get written proof of my employment there.

That employer's website (if available) is _____ .

ABOUT MY PREVIOUS
WORK IN MY NATIVE COUNTRY

Here were my major job responsibilities:

_____
_____
_____
_____

Here were some specific skills that I used on the job (for example, writing reports, training others, operating equipment, and other skills):

_____
_____
_____

I supervised _____ people. (give the number of people)

Any additional important information about my job:

Consider the following when explaining your responsibilities:

- How many similar positions were there at your institution or in your city?
- Was the position created because of your particular talents?

- Did you receive special training or contribute to special training of others?
- Were you the youngest or oldest to hold the position?
- Did the situation in which you were involved have great impact? on whom? (Example: a hospital emergency room's impact on very sick people)
- Other circumstances or details you can think of:

_____

_____

_____

I obtained this position because of a promotion. Circle **YES** or **NO**.

I worked for this last employer during the following dates:

_____

Here are the job titles and dates from my work with **other employers** in my native country. **The most recent date is first.**

_____

_____

_____

Here is how my profession is practiced in my native country compared to the United States.

_____

_____

_____

ABOUT MY MOST RECENT
EMPLOYER IN MY NATIVE COUNTRY

I will describe my last employer (company, agency, place of work) in my native country, since most Americans are not familiar with it.

The type of work this employer performs is_____.

There are _____ people who work for this employer. (give the number of people)

It is a (**PRIVATE** or **PUBLIC**) employer. (circle one)

It is **national, state, local**. (circle as many as apply)

It is a **company, nonprofit organization, educational institution** (circle one)

This employer has _____ clients. (give the number of clients)
   OR
This employer is worth $ _____. (estimate an amount to give the reader an idea of how big the employer is)

MY EDUCATION

My highest level of education is: (circle all those that apply)

elementary school   high school
vocational/trade school special certificate/diploma
college   graduate school   postgraduate

Graduate school name and my specialty area: _____

Diploma or certificate. School name and my specialty:_____

Internship: _____

Honors or awards related to my education or work:

_____
_____

Here is special information I wish to add about my education:

_____
_____

Rather than a formal education, I received most of my knowledge through experience on the job. **YES** or **NO** (circle one)

MY PLANS FOR THE FUTURE

Job Options

I am interested in (check all that apply to you):

_____ resuming my previous profession no matter how long it takes
_____ resuming my previous profession if it does not take too many years
_____ looking into other options using the skills of my profession
_____ becoming an entrepreneur
_____ exploring completely new fields

Mobility

I am willing to relocate within the United States where there might be (write YES or NO in each space):

_____ greater need for my skills
_____ greater retraining options in a field of my interest
_____ greater financial aid in my field of interest

MY HOBBIES

(Your hobbies and interests may help a prospective employer apply your talents to a job opportunity.)

I like the following hobbies. I started them either in my native country or in the United States.

_____

_____

_____

_____

_____

_____

I am proud of my hobby as a _____ (name the specific hobby)
because _____

MY POSITIONS IN THE UNITED STATES

(You will need this information for your resume and for employment
applications.)

Since coming to the United States, I have held the following positions.
The **most recent is first.**

Title/ duties	Dates	Hours/ week	Company	Address	Phone	Supervisor /title	Reason you left
1.							
2.							
3.							
4.							
5.							

Here are three references you can contact about my character. They are
not members of my family. (Give name, address, and phone number.
You may need this information for your employment applications.)

1. _____
2. _____
3. _____

Appendix C

Getting Your Foreign Credentials Evaluated

U.S. schools, as well as employers and license-granting agencies, the U.S. Bureau of Citizenship and Immigration Services—BCIS (formerly U.S. Immigration and Naturalization Service—INS), and others may want to know your foreign educational background. Therefore, these organizations may request an evaluation of your foreign education credentials.

WHAT IS EVALUATED

The evaluation consists of identifying your studies abroad and explaining how such academic work might be comparable to similar studies at U.S. colleges and universities. In addition, organizations in your profession may check to see whether your credentials and courses meet minimum standards of your profession. An example of such an organization is Engineering Credentials Evaluation International.

You may be asked to submit credentials that identify one or more of the following at schools you have attended abroad:

- Each course of study
- Proof of your degrees

WHO EVALUATES YOUR CREDENTIALS

Your foreign credentials may be evaluated by one of the following:

* The institution, government agency, or employer requesting the information
* Your professional association or a designated organization that evaluates credentials for your profession
* A commercial or nonprofit service that evaluates foreign credentials

Using an Outside Agency

If you must find your own evaluation service, check the National Association of Credential Evaluation Services (NACES) for its list of evaluation services at www.naces.org and links to the website of each service. As the association of independent credentials evaluating companies, NACES sets standards for ethical and proper procedures. Its members must meet its standards. Check the NACES standards.

Also consider having your evaluation performed by the American Association of College Registrars and Admissions Officers (AACRAO), online at www.AACRAO.org/credential/individual.htm; Phone: 202-296-3359; E-mail: oies@aacrao.org. AACRAO has a collegial relationship with NACES.

HOW TO START

Gather Information about What You Must Provide

* Ask the requesting licensing board, educational institution, employer, or other requestor whether it has a preferred evaluation service or whether the requestor performs the evaluation.
* Find out specifically what you must provide the evaluation service. Ask whether you must produce documentation for a general (one page) or course-by-course (detailed) evaluation. Make a list of each item you need to give the evaluator.

- Determine cost. A course-by-course evaluation usually costs under $200. This is likely to cover one or more degrees you may have earned. Check to see whether the credentials must be translated into English, and if so, whether the cost includes translation services.
- Check beforehand that the evaluator will return the materials to you by registered or certified mail, even if you must pay an extra fee. Copies of credentials may not be returned to you, unless you specifically make a request.

Be Aware and Beware: Tips for Handling the Evaluation Process

Do not make assumptions! Evaluation services function in various ways—and institutions, licensing boards, other agencies, and employers have their own varying requirements. If you ask beforehand how a particular evaluation service processes your materials and what your institution requires, you will save much time, effort, anxiety, and money.

- Original documents—may be required, but not always.
- Payment—may be required before the evaluation, but not always.
- Time—usually takes ten to fifteen days from the time the service receives all your documents. Some companies provide rush service of five days or even twenty-four hours for an extra fee.
- Evaluation outcome—evaluation from one service does not bind another service. You may try more than one.
- Fraud—all NACES evaluation services will be notified if there is fraud in your submission. Usually AACRAO will also be notified.
- Purpose—tell the evaluation service why you want your credentials evaluated—a job, admission to a particular school, professional state licensing board (which one), U.S. Bureau of Citizenship and Immigration Services (BCIS; formerly INS), or another purpose. The evaluator will be aware of what additional documents you may need to submit, and whether your coursework meets the agency's requirements; the evaluator is aware that institutions and agencies have their own individual requirements. For BCIS purposes, the evaluator will add the appropriate statement.

Note: If you are submitting originals, mail your credentials carefully to the evaluating agency. Send them by overnight service in a cardboard envelope that will not easily bend. If you are not using the U.S. Post Office's overnight service, send your material registered or certified.

Make copies for your files of all the materials you plan to mail for evaluation including corespondence.

Academic Programs in the United States—and How to Find Schools That Offer Them

As you explore education needs for possible careers, consider academic programs offered throughout the United States when such programs are not available in the Washington, D.C., region.*

HOW THIS LIST OF ACADEMIC PROGRAMS THROUGHOUT THE UNITED STATES CAN HELP YOU

You may want to sign up for an academic program to:

- Learn the American philosophy, practice, and jargon regarding your profession.
- Further validate knowledge of your profession for U.S. employment
- Learn a paraprofession in your field or a related field for faster U.S. employment.
- Learn a new profession or paraprofession.

You may explore how such academic programs lead to career opportunities:

- Contact faculty in such programs who might be willing to give you advice.
- Consult a career counselor.
- Check websites in chapter 2 on the career potential of specific academic programs.

*We gratefully acknowledge the cooperation of the U.S. Department of Education in making its list available for this directory. Please note that the list was adapted for purposes of this directory. U.S. Department of Education, National Center for Education Statistics, Classification of Instructional Programs: 2000 Edition. Washington, DC: NCES.

HOW TO FIND SCHOOLS THAT
OFFER PROGRAMS ON THE LIST

Websites

Using one of the websites in this appendix, you will find schools in the United States that offer general programs in which you are interested. For your initial search, try entering program areas that are part of major headings or subheadings on the list in this section.

- U.S. Department of Education—http://NCES.ed.gov/ipeds/cool; click ipedscool
- College Board—http://apps.collegeboard.com/search/advhome.jsp

Books

You may prefer a book rather than a website that identifies a school that offers the programs of interest to you. One example is *College Board, Index of Majors & Graduate Degrees 2003,* 25th ed. Check your public library reference section and commercial bookstores.

ACADEMIC AND OCCUPATIONALLY
SPECIFIC PROGRAMS

Agriculture, Agriculture Operations, and Related Sciences

Agriculture
Agriculture, Agriculture Operations, and Related Sciences, Other
Agricultural and Food Products Processing
Agricultural and Domestic Animal Services
  Animal Training
  Dog/Pet/Animal Grooming
  Equestrian/Equine Studies
Agricultural Business and Management
  Agribusiness/Agricultural Business Operations
  Agricultural Business and Management, General

Agricultural Business and Management, Other
Agricultural Business Technology
Agricultural Economics
Agricultural/Farm Supplies Retailing and Wholesaling
Farm/Farm and Ranch Management
Agricultural Mechanization
  Agricultural Mechanics and Equipment/Machine Technology
  Agricultural Mechanization, General
  Agricultural Mechanization, Other
  Agricultural Power Machinery Operation

Agricultural Production Operations
Agricultural Production Operations, General
Agricultural Production Operations, Other
Animal/Livestock Husbandry and Production
Aquaculture
Crop Production
Dairy Husbandry and Production
Horse Husbandry/Equine Science and Management
Applied Horticulture/Horticultural Business Services
Applied Horticulture/Horicultural Business Services, Other
Applied Horticulture/Horticultural Operations, General Ornamental Horticulture
Floriculture/Floristry Operations and Management
Greenhouse Operations and Management
Landscaping and Groundskeeping
Plant Nursery Operations and Management
Turf and Turfgrass Management
Agricultural Public Services
Agricultural and Extension Education Services
Agricultural Communication/Journalism
Agricultural Public Services, Other
Animal Sciences
Agricultural Animal Breeding

Animal Health
Animal Nutrition
Animal Sciences, General
Animal Sciences, Other
Dairy Science
Livestock Management
Poultry Science
Food Science and Technology
Food Science
Food Science and Technology, Other
Food Technology and Processing
International Agriculture
Plant Sciences
Agricultural and Horticultural Plant Breeding
Agronomy and Crop Science
Horticultural Science
Plant Protection and Integrated Pest Management
Plant Sciences, General
Plant Sciences, Other
Range Science and Management
Soil Sciences
Soil Chemistry and Physics
Soil Microbiology
Soil Science and Agronomy, General
Soil Sciences, Other
Taxidermy/Taxidermist
Agricultural and Domestic Animal Services, Other

Architecture and Related Services

Architectural History and Criticism
Architectural History and Criticism, General
Architectural Technology/Technician
Architecture and Related Services, Other
Architecture (BArch., BA/BS, MArch, MA/MS, PhD)

City/Urban, Community and Regional Planning
Environmental Design
Environmental Design/Architecture
Interior Architecture
Landscape Architecture (BS, BSLA, BLA, MSLA, MLA, PhD)

Area, Ethnic, Cultural, and Gender Studies

Area, Ethnic, Cultural, and Gender Studies, Other
Area Studies
African Studies

American/United States Studies/Civilization
Area Studies, Other
Asian Studies/Civilization

Balkans Studies
Baltic Studies
Canadian Studies
Caribbean Studies
Central/Middle and Eastern European
Studies
Chinese Studies
Commonwealth Studies
East Asian Studies
European Studies/Civilization
French Studies
German Studies
Italian Studies
Japanese Studies
Korean Studies
Latin American Studies
Near and Middle Eastern Studies
Pacific Area/Pacific Rim Studies
Polish Studies
Regional Studies (U.S., Canadian, foreign)
Russian Studies

Scandinavian Studies
Slavic Studies
South Asian Studies
Southeast Asian Studies
Spanish and Iberian Studies
Tibetan Studies
Ukraine Studies
Ural-Altaic and Central Asian Studies
Western European Studies
*Ethnic, Cultural Minority, and Gender
Studies*
African-American/Black Studies
American Indian/Native American
Studies
Asian-American Studies
Ethnic, Cultural Minority, and Gender
Studies, Other
Gay/Lesbian Studies
Hispanic-American, Puerto Rican, and
Mexican-American/Chicano Studies
Women's Studies

Biological and Biomedical Sciences

*Biochemistry, Biophysics and Molecular
Biology*
  Biochemistry
  Biochemistry, Biophysics and Molecu-
  lar Biology, Other
  Biochemistry/Biophysics and Molecu-
  lar Biology
  Biophysics
  Molecular Biochemistry
  Molecular Biology
  Molecular Biophysics
  Photobiology
  Radiation Biology/Radiobiology
  Structural Biology
Biological and Biomedical Sciences, Other
Biology, General
  Biology/Biological Sciences, General
  Biomedical Sciences, General
Biomathematics and Bioinformatics
  Bioinformatics
  Biomathematics and Bioinformatics,

  Other
  Biometry/Biometrics
  Biostatistics
Biotechnology
  Biotechnology
Botany/Plant Biology
  Botany/Plant Biology
  Botany/Plant Biology, Other
  Plant Molecular Biology
  Plant Pathology/Phytopathology
  Plant Physiology
*Cell/Cellular Biology and Anatomical
Sciences*
  Anatomy
  Cell Biology and Anatomy
  Cell/Cellular and Molecular Biology
  Cell/Cellular Biology and Anatomical
  Sciences, Other
  Cell/Cellular Biology and Histology
  Developmental Biology and Embryology
  Neuroanatomy

Ecology, Evolution, Systematics and Population Biology
  Aquatic Biology/Limnology
  Conservation Biology
  Ecology
  Ecology, Evolution, Systematics and Population Biology, Other
  Environmental Biology
  Epidemiology
  Evolutionary Biology
  Marine Biology and Biological Oceanography
  Population Biology
  Systematic Biology/Biological Systematics
Genetics
  Animal Genetics
  Genetics, General
  Genetics, Other
  Human/Medical Genetics
  Microbial and Eukaryotic Genetics
  Molecular Genetics
  Plant Genetics
Microbiological Sciences and Immunology
  Immunology
  Medical Microbiology and Bacteriology
  Microbiological Sciences and Immunology, Other
  Microbiology, General
  Mycology

  Parasitology
  Virology
Pharmacology and Toxicology
  Environmental Toxicology
  Molecular Pharmacology
  Molecular Toxicology
  Neuropharmacology
  Pharmacology
  Pharmacology and Toxicology
  Pharmacology and Toxicology, Other
  Toxicology
Physiology, Pathology and Related Sciences
  Cardiovascular Science
  Cell Physiology
  Endocrinology
  Exercise Physiology
  Molecular Physiology
  Neurobiology and Neurophysiology
  Oncology and Cancer Biology
  Pathology/Experimental Pathology
  Physiology, General
  Physiology, Pathology, and Related Sciences, Other
  Reproductive Biology
  Vision Science/Physiological Optics
Zoology/Animal Biology
  Animal Behavior and Ethology
  Animal Physiology
  Entomology
  Wildlife Biology
  Zoology/Animal Biology, Other

Business, Management, Marketing, and Related Support Services

Accounting and Related Services
  Accounting
  Accounting and Business/Management
  Accounting and Finance
  Accounting and Related Services, Other
  Accounting Technology/Technician and Bookkeeping
  Auditing

Business Administration, Management and Operations
  Business Administration and Management, General
  Business Administration, Management and Operations, Other
  Customer Service Management
  E-Commerce/Electronic Commerce
  Logistics and Materials Management

Non-Profit/Public/Organizational Management
Office Management and Supervision
Operations Management and Supervision
Purchasing, Procurement/Acquisitions and Contracts Management
Transportation/Transportation Management
Business, Management, Marketing, and Related Support Services, Other
Business Operations Support and Assistant Services
  Administrative Assistant and Secretarial Science, General
  Business Operations Support and Secretarial Services, Other
  Business/Office Automation/Technology/Data Entry
  Customer Service Support/Call Center/Teleservice Operation
  Executive Assistant/Executive Secretary
  General Office Occupations and Clerical Services
  Parts, Warehousing, and Inventory Management Operations
  Receptionist
  Traffic, Customs, and Transportation Clerk/Technician
Business/Commerce, General
Business/Corporate Communications
Business/Managerial Economics
Construction Management
Entrepreneurial and Small Business Operations
  Entrepreneurial and Small Business Operations, Other
  Entrepreneurship/Entrepreneurial Studies
  Franchising and Franchise Operations
  Small Business Administration/Management
Finance and Financial Management Services

Banking and Financial Support Services
Credit Management
Finance and Financial Management Services, Other
Finance, General
Financial Planning and Services
International Finance
Investments and Securities
Public Finance
General Sales, Merchandising, and Related Marketing Operations
  General Merchandising, Sales, and Related Marketing Operations, Other
  Merchandising and Buying Operations
  Retailing and Retail Operations
  Sales, Distribution, and Marketing Operations, General
  Selling Skills and Sales Operations
Hospitality Administration/Management
  Hospitality Administration/Management, General
  Hospitality Administration/Management, Other
  Hotel/Motel Administration/Management
  Human Resources Development
  Human Resources Management and Services
  Human Resources Management and Services, Other
  Human Resources Management/Personnel Administration, General
  Labor and Industrial Relations
  Labor Studies
  Organizational Behavior Studies
  Resort Management
  Restaurant/Food Services Management
  Tourism and Travel Services Management
Insurance
International Business
  Information Resources Management/CIO Training
  International Business/Trade/Commerce
  Knowledge Management

Management Information Systems and Services
Management Information Systems and Services, Other
Management Information Systems, General
Management Sciences and Quantitative Methods
Actuarial Science
Business Statistics
Management Science, General
Management Sciences and Quantitative Methods, Other
Marketing
International Marketing
Marketing, Other
Marketing Research
Marketing/Marketing Management, General
Real Estate

Specialized Sales, Merchandising, and Marketing Operations
Apparel and Accessories Marketing Operations
Auctioneering
Business and Personal/Financial Services Marketing Operations
Fashion Merchandising
Fashion Modeling
Hospitality and Recreation Marketing Operations
Special Products Marketing Operations
Specialized Merchandising, Sales, and Related Marketing Operations, Other
Tourism and Travel Services Marketing Operations
Tourism Promotion Operations
Vehicle and Vehicle Parts and Accessories Marketing Operations
Taxation

Communication, Journalism, and Related Programs

Communication and Media Studies
Communication and Media Studies, Other
Communication Studies/Speech Communication and Rhetoric
Mass Communication/Media Studies
Communication, Journalism, and Related Programs, Other
Journalism
Broadcast Journalism
Journalism
Journalism, Other
Photojournalism
Public Relations, Advertising, and Applied Communication

Advertising
Health Communication
Organizational Communication, General
Political Communication
Public Relations, Advertising and Applied Communication, Other
Public Relations/Image Management
Publishing
Radio, Television, and Digital Communication
Digital Communication and Media/Multimedia
Radio and Television
Radio, Television, and Digital Communication, Other

Communications Technologies/ Technicians and Support Services

Audiovisual Communications Technologies/Technicians
Audiovisual Communications Technologies/Technicians, Other

Photographic and Film/Video Technology/Technician and Assistant
Radio and Television Broadcasting Technology/Technician

Recording Arts Technology/Technician
Communications Technologies/Techni-
cians and Support Services, Other
Communications Technology/Technician
Graphic Communications
  Animation, Interactive Technology,
  Video Graphics and Special Effects
  Computer Typography and Composition
  Equipment Operator

Graphic and Printing Equipment Oper-
ator, General Production
Graphic Communications, General
Graphic Communications, Other
Platemaker/Imager
Prepress/Desktop Publishing and Digi-
tal Imaging Design
Printing Management
Printing Press Operator

Computer and Information Sciences and Support Services

Computer and Information Sciences and
Support Services, Other
Computer and Information Sciences, General
  Artificial Intelligence and Robotics
  Computer and Information Sciences,
  General
  Computer and Information Sciences,
  Other
  Information Technology
Computer/Information Technology Ad-
ministration and Management
  Computer and Information Systems
  Security
  Computer/Information Technology
  Services Administration and Manage-
  ment, Other
  System Administration/Administrator
  System, Networking, and LAN/WAN
  Management/Manager
  Web/Multimedia Management and
  Webmaster
Computer Programming
  Computer Programming, Other
  Computer Programming, Specific Ap-
  plications
  Computer Programming,
  Vendor/Product Certification

Computer Programming/
Programmer, General
Computer Science
Computer Software and Media Applica-
tions
  Computer Graphics
  Computer Software and Media Appli-
  cations, Other
  Data Modeling/Warehousing and Data-
  base Administration
  Web Page, Digital/Multimedia and Infor-
  mation Resources Design
Computer Systems Analysis
  Computer Systems Analysis/Analyst
Computer Systems Networking and
Telecommunications
Data Entry/Microcomputer Applications
  Data Entry/Microcomputer Applica-
  tions, General
  Data Entry/Microcomputer Applica-
  tions, Other
  Word Processing
Data Processing
  Data Processing and Data
  Processing Technology/
  Technician
Information Science/Studies

Construction Trades

Building/Construction Finishing, Man-
agement, and Inspection
  Building/Construction Finishing, Manage-
  ment, and Inspection, Other
  Building/Construction Site
  Management/Manager

Building/Home/Construction
Inspection/Inspector
Building/Property Maintenance and
Management
Concrete Finishing/Concrete Finisher
Drywall Installation/Drywaller

Glazier
Metal Building Assembly/Assembler
Painting/Painter and Wall Coverer
Roofer
Carpenters
Carpentry/Carpenter
Construction Trades, General
Construction Trades, Other
Electrical and Power Transmission Installers
Electrical and Power Transmission Installation/Installer, General
Electrical and Power Transmission Installers, Other
Electrician
Lineworker
Mason/Masonry
Plumbing and Related Water Supply Services
Blasting/Blaster
Pipefitting/Pipefitter and Sprinkler Fitter
Plumbing and Related Water Supply Services, Other
Plumbing Technology/Plumber
Well Drilling/Driller

Education

Bilingual, Multilingual, and Multicultural Education
Bilingual and Multilingual Education
Bilingual, Multilingual, and Multicultural Education, Other
Indian/Native American Education
Multicultural Education
Curriculum and Instruction
Education, General
Education, Other
Educational Administration and Supervision
Administration of Special Education
Adult and Continuing Education Administration
Community College Education
Educational Administration and Supervision, Other
Educational, Instructional, and Curriculum Supervision
Educational Leadership and Administration, General
Elementary and Middle School Administration/Principalship
Higher Education/Higher Education Administration
Secondary School Administration/Principalship
Superintendency and Educational System Administration
Urban Education and Leadership

Educational Assessment, Evaluation, and Research
Educational Assessment, Evaluation, and Research, Other
Educational Assessment, Testing, and Measurement
Educational Evaluation and Research
Educational Statistics and Research Methods
Educational/Instructional Media Design
International and Comparative Education
Social and Philosophical Foundations of Education
Special Education and Teaching
Education/Teaching of Individuals in Early Childhood Special Education Programs
Education/Teaching of Individuals Who are Developmentally Delayed
Education/Teaching of Individuals with Autism
Education/Teaching of Individuals with Emotional Disturbances
Education/Teaching of Individuals with Hearing Impairments, Including Deafness
Education/Teaching of Individuals with Mental Retardation
Education/Teaching of Individuals with Multiple Disabilities

Education/Teaching of Individuals with Orthopedic and Other Physical Health Impairments
Education/Teaching of Individuals with Specific Learning Disabilities
Education/Teaching of Individuals with Speech or Language Impairments
Education/Teaching of Individuals with Traumatic Brain Injuries
Education/Teaching of Individuals with Vision Impairments, Including Blindness
Education/Teaching of the Gifted and Talented
Special Education and Teaching, General
Special Education and Teaching, Other

Student Counseling and Personnel Services

College Student Counseling and Personnel Services
Counselor Education/School Counseling and Guidance Services
Student Counseling and Personnel Services, Other

Teacher Education and Professional Development, Specific Levels and Methods

Adult and Continuing Education and Teaching
Early Childhood Education and Teaching
Elementary Education and Teaching
Junior High/Intermediate/Middle School Education and Teaching
Kindergarten/Preschool Education and Teaching
Montessori Teacher Education
Secondary Education and Teaching
Teacher Education and Professional Development, Specific Levels and Methods, Other
Teacher Education, Multiple Levels
Waldorf/Steiner Teacher Education

Teacher Education and Professional Development, Specific Subject Areas

Agricultural Teacher Education
Art Teacher Education
Biology Teacher Education
Business Teacher Education
Chemistry Teacher Education
Computer Teacher Education
Drama and Dance Teacher Education
Driver and Safety Teacher Education
English/Language Arts Teacher Education
Family and Consumer Sciences/Home Economics Teacher Education
Foreign Language Teacher Education
French Language Teacher Education
Geography Teacher Education
German Language Teacher Education
Health Occupations Teacher Education
Health Teacher Education
History Teacher Education
Latin Teacher Education
Mathematics Teacher Education
Music Teacher Education
Physical Education Teaching and Coaching
Physics Teacher Education
Psychology Teacher Education
Reading Teacher Education
Sales and Marketing Operations/Marketing and Distribution Teacher Education
School Librarian/School Library Media Specialist
Science Teacher Education/General
Science Teacher Education
Social Science Teacher Education
Spanish Language Teacher Education
Speech Teacher Education
Teacher Education and Professional Development, Specific Subject Areas, Other
Technical Teacher Education
Technology Teacher Education/Industrial Arts Teacher Education
Trade and Industrial Teacher Education

Teaching Assistants/Aides
Adult Literacy Tutor/Instructor
Teacher Assistant/Aide
Teaching Assistants/Aides, Other
Teaching English or French as a Second or Foreign Language

Teaching English as a Second or Foreign Language/ESL Language Instructor
Teaching English or French as a Second or Foreign Language, Other
Teaching French as a Second or Foreign Language

Engineering

Aerospace, Aeronautical and Astronautical Engineering
Agricultural/Biological Engineering and Bioengineering
Architectural Engineering
Biomedical/Medical Engineering
Ceramic Sciences and Engineering
Chemical Engineering
Civil Engineering
Civil Engineering, General
Civil Engineering, Other
Geotechnical Engineering
Structural Engineering
Transportation and Highway Engineering
Water Resources Engineering
Computer Engineering, General
Computer Engineering, General
Computer Engineering, Other
Computer Hardware Engineering
Computer Software Engineering
Construction Engineering
Electrical, Electronics and Communications Engineering
Engineering, General

Engineering Mechanics
Engineering, Other
Engineering Physics
Engineering Science
Environmental/Environmental Health Engineering
Forest Engineering
Geological/Geophysical Engineering
Industrial Engineering
Manufacturing Engineering
Materials Engineering
Materials Science
Mechanical Engineering
Metallurgical Engineering
Mining and Mineral Engineering
Naval Architecture and Marine Engineering
Nuclear Engineering
Ocean Engineering
Operations Research
Petroleum Engineering
Polymer/Plastics Engineering
Surveying Engineering
Systems Engineering
Textile Sciences and Engineering

Engineering Technologies/Technicians

Architectural Engineering Technologies/Technicians
Civil Engineering Technologies/Technicians
Computer Engineering Technologies/Technicians
Computer Engineering Technologies/Technicians, Other
Computer Engineering Technology/Technician

Computer Hardware Technology/Technician
Computer Software Technology/Technician
Computer Technology/Computer Systems Technology
Construction Engineering Technologies
Drafting/Design Engineering Technologies/Technicians
Architectural Drafting and Architectural CAD/CADD

CAD/CADD Drafting and/or Design Technology/Technician

Civil Drafting and Civil Engineering CAD/CADD

Drafting and Design Technology/Technician, General

Drafting/Design Engineering Technologies/Technicians, Other

Electrical/Electronics Drafting and Electrical/Electronics CAD/CADD

Mechanical Drafting and Mechanical Drafting CAD/CADD

Electrical Engineering Technologies/Technicians

Electrical and Electronic Engineering Technologies/Technicians, Other

Electrical, Electronic and Communications Engineering Technology/Technician

Laser and Optical Technology/Technician

Telecommunications Technology/Technician

Electromechanical Instrumentation and Maintenance Technologies/Technicians

Biomedical Technology/Technician

Electromechanical and Instrumentation and Maintenance Technologies/Technicians, Other

Electromechanical Technology/Electromechanical Engineering Technology

Instrumentation Technology/Technician

Robotics Technology/Technician

Engineering Technologies/Technicians, Other

Engineering Technology, General

Engineering-Related Fields

Engineering/Industrial Management

Engineering-Related Technologies

Engineering-Related Technologies, Other

Hydraulics and Fluid Power Technology/Technician

Surveying Technology/Surveying

Environmental Control Technologies/Technicians

Energy Management and Systems Technology/Technician

Environmental Control Technologies/Technicians, Other

Environmental Engineering Technology/Environmental Technology

Hazardous Materials Management and Waste Technology/Technician

Heating, Air Conditioning and Refrigeration Technology/Technician (ACH/ACR/ACHR/HRAC/HVAC/AC Technology)

Solar Energy Technology/Technician

Water Quality and Wastewater Treatment Management and Recycling Technology/Technician

Industrial Production Technologies/Technicians

Industrial Production Technologies/Technicians, Other

Industrial Technology/Technician

Manufacturing Technology/Technician

Metallurgical Technology/Technician

Plastics Engineering Technology/Technician

Mechanical Engineering Related Technologies/Technicians

Aeronautical/Aerospace Engineering Technology/Technician

Automotive Engineering Technology/Technician

Mechanical Engineering Related Technologies/Technicians, Other

Mechanical Engineering/Mechanical Technology/Technician

Mining and Petroleum Technologies/Technicians

Mining and Petroleum Technologies/Technicians, Other

Mining Technology/Technician

Petroleum Technology/Technician

Nuclear Engineering Technologies/Technicians

Quality Control and Safety Technologies/Technicians

Hazardous Materials Information Systems Technology/Technician

Industrial Safety Technology/Technician
Occupational Safety and Health Technology/Technician

Quality Control and Safety Technologies/Technicians, Other
Quality Control Technology/Technician

English Language and Literature/Letters

American Literature (United States and Canadian)
   American Literature (United States)
   American Literature (Canadian)
Creative Writing
English Composition
English Language and Literature, General

English Language and Literature/Letters, Other
English Literature (British and Commonwealth)
Speech and Rhetorical Studies
Technical and Business Writing

Family and Consumer Sciences/Human Sciences

Apparel and Textiles
   Apparel and Textile Manufacture
   Apparel and Textile Marketing Management
   Apparel and Textiles, General
   Apparel and Textiles, Other
   Fashion and Fabric Consultant
   Textile Science
Family and Consumer Economics and Related Studies
   Consumer Economics
   Consumer Services and Advocacy
   Family and Consumer Economics and Related Services, Other
   Family Resource Management Studies, General
Family and Consumer Sciences/ Human Sciences Business Services
   Business Family and Consumer Sciences/Human Sciences
   Consumer Merchandising/Retailing Management
   Family and Consumer Sciences/Human Sciences Business Services, Other
   Family and Consumer Sciences/Human Sciences Communication
Family and Consumer Sciences/Human Sciences, General
Family and Consumer Sciences/Human Sciences, Other

Foods, Nutrition, and Related Services
   Foods, Nutrition, and Related Services, Other
   Foods, Nutrition, and Wellness Studies, General
   Foodservice Systems Administration/Management
   Human Nutrition
Housing and Human Environments
   Facilities Planning and Management
   Home Furnishings and Equipment Installers
   Housing and Human Environments, General
   Housing and Human Environments, Other
Human Development, Family Studies, and Related Services
   Adult Development and Aging
   Child Care and Support Services Management
   Child Care Provider/Assistant
   Child Development
   Family and Community Services
   Family Systems
   Human Development and Family Studies, General
   Human Development, Family Studies, and Related Services, Other
Work and Family Studies

Foreign Languages, Literatures, and Linguistics

African Languages, Literatures, and Linguistics

American Indian/Native American Languages, Literatures, and Linguistics

American Sign Language (ASL)
  American Sign Language (ASL)
  American Sign Language, Other
  Linguistics of ASL and Other Sign Languages
  Sign Language Interpretation and Translation

Celtic Languages, Literatures, and Linguistics

Classics and Classical Languages, Literatures, and Linguistics
  Ancient/Classical Greek Language and Literature
  Classics and Classical Languages, Literatures, and Linguistics, General
  Classics and Classical Languages, Literatures, and Linguistics, Other
  Latin Language and Literature

East Asian Languages, Literatures, and Linguistics
  Chinese Language and Literature
  East Asian Languages, Literatures, and Linguistics, General
  East Asian Languages, Literatures, and Linguistics, Other
  Japanese Language and Literature
  Korean Language and Literature
  Tibetan Language and Literature

Foreign Languages, Literatures, and Linguistics, Other

Germanic Languages, Literatures, and Linguistics
  Danish Language and Literature
  Dutch/Flemish Language and Literature
  German Language and Literature
  Germanic Languages, Literatures, and Linguistics, General
  Germanic Languages, Literatures, and Linguistics, Other

Norwegian Language and Literature

Scandinavian Languages, Literatures, and Linguistics

Swedish Language and Literature

Iranian/Persian Languages, Literatures, and Linguistics

Linguistics Comparative, and Related Language Studies and Services
  Comparative Literature
  Foreign Languages and Literatures, General
  Language Interpretation and Translation
  Linguistic, Comparative, and Related Language Studies and Services, Other
  Linguistics

Middle/Near Eastern and Semitic Languages, Literatures, and Linguistics
  Ancient Near Eastern and Biblical Languages, Literatures, and Linguistics
  Arabic Language and Literature
  Hebrew Language and Literature
  Middle/Near Eastern and Semitic Languages, Literatures, and Linguistics, Other
  Semitic Languages, Literatures, and Linguistics, General

Modern Greek Language and Literature

Romance Languages, Literatures, and Linguistics
  Catalan Language and Literature
  French Language and Literature
  Italian Language and Literature
  Portuguese Language and Literature
  Romance Languages, Literatures, and Linguistics, General
  Romance Languages, Literatures, and Linguistics, Other
  Romanian Language and Literature
  Spanish Language and Literature

Slavic, Baltic and Albanian Languages, Literatures, and Linguistics
  Albanian Language and Literature
  Baltic Languages, Literatures, and Linguistics

Bulgarian Language and Literature
Czech Language and Literature
Polish Language and Literature
Russian Language and Literature
Serbian, Croatian, and Serbo-Croatian Languages and Literatures
Slavic, Baltic, and Albanian Languages, Literatures, and Linguistics, Other
Slavic Languages, Literatures, and Linguistics, General
Slovak Language and Literature
Ukrainian Language and Literature
South Asian Languages, Literatures, and Linguistics
Bengali Language and Literature
Hindi Language and Literature
Panjabi Language and Literature
Sanskrit and Classical Indian Languages, Literatures, and Linguistics
South Asian Languages, Literatures, and Linguistics, General
South Asian Languages, Literatures, and Linguistics, Other
Tamil Language and Literature
Urdu Language and Literature
Southeast Asian and Australasian/Pacific Languages, Literatures, and Linguistics

Australian/Oceanic/Pacific Languages, Literatures, and Linguistics
Bahasa Indonesian/Bahasa Malay Languages and Literatures
Burmese Language and Literature
Filipino/Tagalog Language and Literature
Khmer/Cambodian Language and Literature
Lao/Laotian Language and Literature
Southeast Asian and Australasian/Pacific Languages, Literatures, and Linguistics, Other
Southeast Asian Languages, Literatures, and Linguistics, General
Thai Language and Literature
Vietnamese Language and Literature
Turkic, Ural-Altaic, Caucasian, and Central Asian Languages, Literatures, and Linguistics
Finnish and Related Languages, Literatures, and Linguistics
Hungarian/Magyar Language and Literature
Mongolian Language and Literature
Turkic, Ural-Altaic, Caucasian, and Central Asian Languages, Literatures, and Linguistics, Other
Turkish Language and Literature

Health Professions and Related Clinical Sciences

Allied Health and Medical Assisting Services
Allied Health and Medical Assisting Services, Other
Anesthesiologist Assistant
Chiropractic Assistant/Technician
Clinical/Medical Laboratory Assistant
Emergency Care Attendant (EMT Ambulance)
Medical/Clinical Assistant
Occupational Therapist Assistant
Pathology/Pathologist Assistant
Pharmacy Technician/Assistant
Physical Therapist Assistant

Respiratory Therapy Technician/Assistant
Veterinary/Animal Health Technology/Technician and Veterinary Assistant
Allied Health Diagnostic, Intervention, and Treatment Professions
Allied Health Diagnostic, Intervention, and Treatment Professions, Other
Athletic Training/Trainer
Cardiopulmonary Technology/Technologist
Cardiovascular Technology/Technologist

Diagnostic Medical Sonography/Sonographer and Ultrasound Technician
Electrocardiograph Technology/Technician
Electroneurodiagnostic/Electroencephalographic Technology/Technologist
Emergency Medical Technology/Technician (EMT Paramedic)
Gene/Genetic Therapy
Medical Radiologic Technology/Science: Radiation Therapist
Nuclear Medical Technology/Technologist
Perfusion Technology/Perfusionist
Physician Assistant
Radiation Protection/Health Physics Technician
Radiologic Technology/Science: Radiographer
Respiratory Care Therapy/Therapist
Surgical Technology/Technologist
Alternative and Complementary Medical Support Services
Alternative and Complementary Medical Support Services, Other
Direct Entry Midwifery (LM, CPM)
Alternative and Complementary Medicine and Medical Systems
Acupuncture
Alternative and Complementary Medicine and Medical Systems, Other
Ayurvedic Medicine/Ayurveda
Homeopathic Medicine/Homeopathy
Naturopathic Medicine/Naturopathy (ND)
Traditional Chinese/Asian Medicine and Chinese Herbology
Bioethics/Medical Ethics
Chiropractic (DC)
Clinical/Medical Laboratory Science and Allied Professions
Blood Bank Technology Specialist
Clinical Laboratory Science/Medical Technology/Technologist
Clinical/Medical Laboratory Science and Allied Professions, Other

Clinical/Medical Laboratory Technician
Cytogenetics/Genetics/Clinical Genetics Technology/Technologist
Cytotechnology/Cytotechnologist
Hematology Technology/Technician
Histologic Technician
Histologic Technology/Histotechnologist
Ophthalmic Laboratory Technology/Technician
Phlebotomy/Phlebotomist
Renal/Dialysis Technologist/Technician
Communication Disorders Sciences and Services
Audiology/Audiologist and Hearing Sciences
Audiology/Audiologist and Speech-Language Pathology/Pathologist
Communication Disorders, General
Communication Disorders Sciences and Services, Other
Speech-Language Pathology/Pathologist
Dental Support Services and Allied Professions
Dental Assisting/Assistant
Dental Hygiene/Hygienist
Dental Laboratory Technology/Technician
Dental Services and Allied Professions, Other
Dentistry (DDS, DMD)Advanced/Graduate Dentistry and Oral Sciences (Cert, MS, PhD)
Advanced General Dentistry (Cert, MS, PhD)
Advanced/Graduate Dentistry and Oral Sciences, Other
Dental Clinical Sciences, General (MS, PhD)
Dental Materials (MS, PhD)
Dental Public Health and Education (Cert, MS/MPH, PhD/DPH)
Endodontics/Endodontology (Cert, MS, PhD)

Oral Biology and Oral Pathology (MS, PhD)

Oral/Maxillofacial Surgery (Cert, MS, PhD)

Orthodontics/Orthodontology (Cert, MS, PhD)

Pediatric Dentistry/Pedodontics (Cert, MS, PhD)

Periodontics/Periodontology (Cert, MS, PhD)

Prosthodontics/Prosthodontology (Cert, MS, PhD)

Dietetics and Clinical Nutrition Services

Clinical Nutrition/Nutritionist

Dietetic Technician (DTR)

Dietetics and Clinical Nutrition Services, Other

Dietetics/Dietitian (RD)

Dietitian Assistant

Energy and Biologically Based Therapies

Aromatherapy

Energy and Biologically Based Therapies, Other

Herbalism/Herbalist

Polarity Therapy

Reiki

Health Aides/Attendants/ Orderlies

Health Aide

Health Aides/Attendants/Orderlies, Other

Home Health Aide/Home Attendant

Medication Aide

Health and Medical Administrative Services

Health and Medical Administrative Services, Other

Health Information/Medical Records Administration/Administrator

Health Information/Medical Records Technology/Technician

Health Unit Coordinator/Ward Clerk

Health Unit Manager/Ward Supervisor

Health/Health Care Administration/Management

Health/Medical Claims Examiner

Hospital and Health Care Facilities Administration/Management

Medical Administrative/Executive Assistant and Medical Secretary

Medical Insurance Coding Specialist/Coder

Medical Insurance Specialist/Medical Biller

Medical Office Assistant/Specialist

Medical Office Computer Specialist/Assistant

Medical Office Management/Administration

Medical Reception/Receptionist

Medical Staff Services Technology/Technician

Medical Transcription/Transcriptionist

Medical/Health Management and Clinical Assistant/Specialist

Health Professions and Related Clinical Sciences, Other

Health Services/Allied Health/Health Sciences, General

Health/Medical Preparatory Programs

Health/Medical Preparatory Programs, Other

Pre-Dentistry Studies

Pre-Medicine/Pre-Medical Studies

Pre-Nursing Studies

Pre-Pharmacy Studies

Pre-Veterinary Studies

Medical Clinical Sciences/Graduate Medical Studies

Medical Scientist (MS, PhD)

Medical Illustration and Informatics

Medical Illustration and Informatics, Other

Medical Illustration/Medical Illustrator

Medical Informatics

Medicine (MD)

Mental and Social Health Services and Allied Professions

Clinical Pastoral Counseling/Patient Counseling

Clinical/Medical Social Work

Community Health Services/
Liaison/Counseling
Genetic Counseling/Counselor
Marriage and Family Therapy/Coun-
seling
Mental and Social Health Services and
Allied Professions, Other
Mental Health Counseling/Counselor
Psychiatric/Mental Health Services
Technician
Psychoanalysis and Psychotherapy
Substance Abuse/Addiction Counseling
*Movement and Mind-Body Therapies and
Education*
Hypnotherapy/Hypnotherapist
Movement and Mind-Body Therapies
and Education, Other
Movement Therapy and Movement
Education
Yoga Teacher Training/Yoga Therapy
Nursing
Adult Health Nurse/Nursing
Clinical Nurse Specialist
Critical Care Nursing
Family Practice Nurse/Nurse Practi-
tioner
Licensed Practical /Vocational Nurse
Training (LPN, LVN, Cert, Dipl, AAS)
Maternal/Child Health and Neonatal
Nurse/Nursing
Nurse Anesthetist
Nurse Midwife/Nursing Midwifery
Nurse/Nursing Assistant/Aide and Pa-
tient Care Assistant
Nursing Administration (MSN, MS,
PhD)
Nursing, Other
Nursing: Registered Nurse Training
(RN, ASN, BSN, MSN)
Nursing Science (MS, PhD)
Occupational and Environmental
Health Nursing
Pediatric Nurse/Nursing
Perioperative/Operating Room and
Surgical Nurse/Nursing
Psychiatric/Mental Health Nurse/Nursing

Public Health/Community Nurse/Nurs-
ing
*Ophthalmic and Optometric Support Ser-
vices and Allied Professions*
Ophthalmic and Optometric Support
Services and Allied Professions, Other
Ophthalmic Technician/Technologist
Opticianry/Ophthalmic Dispensing Op-
tician
Optomeric Technician/Assistant
Orthoptics/Orthoptist
Optometry (OD)
Osteopathic Medicine/Osteopathy (DO)
*Pharmacy, Pharmaceutical Sciences, and
Administration*
Clinical and Industrial Drug Develop-
ment (MS, PhD)
Clinical, Hospital, and Managed Care
Pharmacy (MS, PhD)
Industrial and Physical Pharmacy and
Cosmetic Sciences (MS, PhD)
Medicinal and Pharmaceutical Chem-
istry (MS, PhD)
Natural Products Chemistry and Phar-
macognosy (MS, PhD)
Pharmaceutics and Drug Design (MS,
PhD)
Pharmacoeconomics/Pharmaceutical
Economics (MS, PhD)
Pharmacy Administration and Phar-
macy Policy and Regulatory Affairs
(MS, PhD)
Pharmacy, Pharmaceutical Sciences,
and Administration, Other
Pharmacy (PharmD [USA] PharmD,
BS/BPharm [Canada])
Podiatric Medicine/Podiatry (DPM)
Public Health
Community Health and Preventive
Medicine
Environmental Health
Health Services Administration
Health/Medical Physics
International Public Health/Interna-
tional Health
Maternal and Child Health

Occupational Health and Industrial Hygiene
Public Health Education and Promotion
Public Health, General (MPH, DPH)
Public Health, Other
Rehabilitation and Therapeutic Professions
  Art Therapy/Therapist
  Assistive/Augmentative Technology and Rehabiliation Engineering
  Dance Therapy/Therapist
  Kinesiotherapy/Kinesiotherapist
  Music Therapy/Therapist
  Occupational Therapy/Therapist
  Orthotist/Prosthetist
  Physical Therapy/Therapist
  Rehabilitation and Therapeutic Professions, Other
  Therapeutic Recreation/Recreational Therapy
  Vocational Rehabilitation Counseling/Counselor
Somatic Bodywork and Related Therapeutic Services
  Asian Bodywork Therapy
  Massage Therapy/Therapeutic Massage
  Somatic Bodywork

Somatic Bodywork and Related Therapeutic Services, Other
Veterinary Biomedical and Clinical Sciences (Cert, MS, PhD)
  Comparative and Laboratory Animal Medicine (Cert, MS, PhD)
  Large Animal/Food Animal and Equine Surgery and Medicine (Cert, MS, PhD)
  Small/Companion Animal Surgery and Medicine (Cert, MS, PhD)
  Veterinary Anatomy (Cert, MS, PhD)
  Veterinary Biomedical and Clinical Sciences, Other (Cert, MS PhD)
  Veterinary Infectious Diseases (Cert, MS, PhD)
  Veterinary Microbiology and Immunobiology (Cert, MS, PhD)
  Veterinary Pathology and Pathobiology (Cert, MS, PhD)
  Veterinary Physiology (Cert, MS, PhD)
  Veterinary Preventive Medicine Epidemiology and Public Health (Cert, MS, PhD)
  Veterinary Sciences/Veterinary Clinical Sciences, General (Cert, MS, PhD)
  Veterinary Toxicology and Pharmacology (Cert, MS, PhD)
Veterinary Medicine (DVM)

History

American History (United States)
Asian History
Canadian History
European History
History and Philosophy of Science and Technology

History, General
History, Other
Public/Applied History and Archival Administration

Legal Professions and Studies

Law (LLB, JD)
Legal Professions and Studies, Other
Legal Research and Advanced Professional Studies (Post-LLB/JD)
  Advanced Legal Research/Studies, General (LLM, MCL, MLI, MSL, JSD/SJD)

American/US Law/Legal Studies/Jurisprudence (LLM, MCJ, JSD/SJD)
Banking, Corporate, Finance, and Securities Law (LLM, JSD/SJD)
Canadian Law/Legal Studies/Jurisprudence (LLM, MCJ, JSD/SJD)
Comparative Law (LLM, MCL, JSD/SJD)

Energy, Environment, and Natural Re-
sources Law (LLM, MS, JSD/SJD)
Health Law (LLM, MJ, JSD/SJD)
International Business, Trade, and Tax
Law (LLM, JSD/SJD)
International Law and Legal Studies
(LLM, JSD/SJD)
Legal Research and Advanced Profes-
sional Studies, Other
Programs for Foreign Lawyers (LLM,
MCL)

Tax Law/Taxation (LLM, JSD/SJD)
Legal Support Services
Court Reporting/Court Reporter
Legal Administrative Assistant/Secre-
tary
Legal Assistant/Paralegal
Legal Support Services, Other
Non-Professional General Legal Studies
(undergraduate)
Legal Studies, General
Pre-Law Studies

Liberal Arts and Sciences, General Studies, and Humanities

Liberal Arts and Sciences, General Stud-
ies, and Humanities
General Studies
Humanities/Humanistic Studies

Liberal Arts and Sciences, General Stud-
ies and Humanities, Other
Liberal Arts and Sciences/Liberal
Studies

Library Science

Library Assistant
Library Assistant/Technician

Library Science, Other
Library Science/Librarianship

Mathematics and Statistics

Applied Mathematics
Applied Mathematics, General
Applied Mathematics, Other
Computational Mathematics
Mathematics
Algebra and Number Theory
Analysis and Functional Analysis
Geometry/Geometric Analysis

Mathematics, General
Mathematics, Other
Topology and Foundations
Mathematics and Statistics, Other
Statistics
Mathematical Statistics and Probability
Statistics, General
Statistics, Other

Mechanic and Repair Technologies/Technicians

Electrical/Electronics Maintenance and
Repair Technology
Appliance Installation and Repair
Technology/Technician
Business Machine Repair
Communications Systems Installation
and Repair Technology
Computer Installation and Repair Tech-
nology/Technician
Electrical/Electronics Equipment In-
stallation and Repair, General

Electrical/Electronics Maintenance and
Repair Technology, Other
Industrial Electronics
Technology/Technician
Security System Installation, Repair,
and Inspection Technology/
Technician
Heating, Air Conditioning, Ventilation
and Refrigeration Maintenance Technol-
ogy/Technician (HAC, HACR, HVAC,
HVACR)

Heavy Equipment Maintenance Technology/Technician
Heavy/Industrial Equipment Maintenance Technologies
Heavy/Industrial Equipment Maintenance Technologies, Other
Industrial Mechanics and Maintenance Technology
Mechanic and Repair Technologies/Technicians, Other
Mechanics and Repairers, General
Precision Systems Maintenance and Repair Technologies
Gunsmithing/Gunsmith
Locksmithing and Safe Repair
Musical Instrument Fabrication and Repair
Parts and Warehousing Operations and Maintenance Technology/Technician
Precision Systems Maintenance and Repair Technologies, Other
Watchmaking and Jewelrymaking
Vehicle Maintenance and Repair Technologies
Aircraft Powerplant Technology/Technician

Airframe Mechanics and Aircraft Maintenance Technology/Technician
Alternative Fuel Vehicle Technology/Technician
Autobody/Collision and Repair Technology/Technician
Automobile/Automotive Mechanics Technology/Technician
Avionics Maintenance Technology/Technician
Bicycle Mechanics and Repair Technology/Technician
Diesel Mechanics Technology/Technician
Engine Machinist
Marine Maintenance/Fitter and Ship Repair Technology/Technician
Medium/Heavy Vehicle and Truck Technology/Technician
Motorcycle Maintenance and Repair Technology/Technician
Small Engine Mechanics and Repair Technology/Technician
Vehicle Emissions Inspection and Maintenance Technology/Technician
Vehicle Maintenance and Repair Technologies, Other

Military Technologies

Multi/Interdisciplinary Studies

Accounting and Computer Science
Behavioral Sciences
Biological and Physical Sciences
Biopsychology
Classical and Ancient Studies
Ancient Studies/Civilization
Classical, Ancient Mediterranean, and Near Eastern Studies and Archaeology
Cognitive Science
Multi/Interdisciplinary Studies, Other
Gerontology
Historic Preservation and Conservation
Cultural Resource Management and Policy Analysis

Historic Preservation and Conservation, Other
Holocaust and Related Studies
Intercultural/Multicultural and Diversity Studies
International/Global Studies
Mathematics and Computer Science
Medieval and Renaissance Studies
Museology/Museum Studies
Natural Sciences
Neuroscience
Nutrition Sciences
Peace Studies and Conflict Resolution
Science, Technology and Society
Systems Science and Theory

Natural Resources and Conservation

Fishing and Fisheries Sciences and Management
Forestry
  Forest Management/Forest Resources Management
  Forest Resources Production and Management
  Forest Sciences and Biology
  Forest Technology/Technician
  Forestry, General
  Forestry, Other
  Urban Forestry
  Wood Science and Wood Products/Pulp and Paper Technology
Natural Resources and Conservation, Other
Natural Resources Conservation and Research
Environmental Science
Environmental Studies
Natural Resources Conservation and Research, Other
Natural Resources/Conservation, General
Natural Resources Management and Policy
  Land Use Planning and Management/Development
  Natural Resource Economics
  Natural Resources Management and Policy, Other
  Water, Wetlands, and Marine Resources Management
Wildlife and Wildlands Science and Management

Parks, Recreation, Leisure, and Fitness Studies

Health and Physical Education/Fitness
  Health and Physical Education, General
  Health and Physical Education/Fitness, Other
  Kinesiology and Exercise Science
Sport and Fitness Administration/Management
Parks, Recreation, and Leisure Facilities Management
Parks, Recreation, and Leisure Studies
Parks, Recreation, Leisure, and Fitness Studies, Other

Personal and Culinary Services

Cosmetology and Related Personal Grooming Services
  Aesthetician/Esthetician and Skin Care Specialist
  Barbering/Barber
  Cosmetology and Related Personal Grooming Arts, Other
  Cosmetology, Barber/Styling, and Nail Instructor
  Cosmetology/Cosmetologist, General
  Electrolysis/Electrology and Electrolysis Technician
  Facial Treatment Specialist/Facialist
  Hair Styling/Stylist and Hair Design
  Make-Up Artist/Specialist
Nail Technician/Specialist and Manicurist
Permanent Cosmetics/Makeup and Tattooing
Salon/Beauty Salon Management/Manager
Culinary Arts and Related Services
  Baking and Pastry Arts/Baker/Pastry Chef
  Bartending/Bartender
  Cooking and Related Culinary Arts, General
  Culinary Arts and Related Services, Other
  Culinary Arts/Chef Training

Food Preparation/Professional Cooking/Kitchen Assistant

Food Service, Waiter/Waitress, and
Dining Room Management/Manager
Institutional Food Workers
Meat Cutting/Meat Cutter
Restaurant, Culinary, and Catering
Management/Manager
Funeral Service and Mortuary Science
Funeral Direction/Service

Funeral Service and Mortuary Science,
General
Funeral Service and Mortuary Science,
Other
Mortuary Science and Embalming/
Embalmer
Personal and Culinary Services, Other

Philosophy and Religious Studies

Philosophy
Ethics
Logic
Philosophy, General
Philosophy, Other
Philosophy and Religious Studies,
Other

Religion/Religious Studies
Buddhist Studies
Christian Studies
Hindu Studies
Islamic Studies
Jewish/Judaic Studies
Religion/Religious Studies, Other

Physical Sciences

Astronomy and Astrophysics
Astronomy
Astronomy and Astrophysics, Other
Astrophysics
Planetary Astronomy and Science
Atmospheric Sciences and Meteorology
Atmospheric Chemistry and Climatology
Atmospheric Physics and Dynamics
Atmospheric Sciences and Meteorol-
ogy, General
Atmospheric Sciences and Meteorol-
ogy, Other
Meteorology
Chemistry
Analytical Chemistry
Chemical Physics
Chemistry, General
Chemistry, Other
Inorganic Chemistry
Organic Chemistry
Physical and Theoretical Chemistry
Polymer Chemistry
Geological and Earth Sciences/
Geosciences

Geochemistry
Geochemistry and Petrology
Geological and Earth Sciences/Geo-
sciences, Other
Geology/Earth Science, General
Geophysics and Seismology
Hydrology and Water Resources Sci-
ence
Oceanography, Chemical and Physical
Paleontology
Physical Sciences
Physical Sciences, Other
Physics
Acoustics
Atomic/Molecular Physics
Elementary Particle Physics
Nuclear Physics
Optics/Optical Sciences
Physics, General
Physics, Other
Plasma and High-Temperature Physics
Solid State and Low-Temperature
Physics
Theoretical and Mathematical Physics

Precision Production

Boilermaking/Boilermaker
Leatherworking and Upholstery
  Leatherworking and Upholstery, Other
  Shoe, Boot and Leather Repair
  Upholstery/Upholsterer
Precision Metal Working
  Ironworking/Ironworker
  Machine Shop Technology/Assistant
  Machine Tool Technology/Machinist
  Precision Metal Working, Other

  Sheet Metal Technology/Sheetworking
  Tool and Die Technology/Technician
  Welding Technology/Welder
Precision Production, Other
Precision Production Trades, General
Woodworking
  Cabinetmaking and Millwork/Millwright
  Furniture Design and Manufacturing
  Woodworking, General
  Woodworking, Other

Psychology

Clinical Child Psychology
Clinical Psychology
Cognitive Psychology and Psycholinguistics
Community Psychology
Comparative Psychology
Counseling Psychology
Developmental and Child Psychology
Educational Psychology
Environmental Psychology
Experimental Psychology
Family Psychology
Forensic Psychology

Geropsychology
Health Psychology
  Health/Medical Psychology
Industrial and Organizational Psychology
Personality Psychology
Physiological Psychology/Psychobiology
Psychology, General
Psychology, Other
Psychometrics and Quantitative Psychology
Psychopharmacology
School Psychology
Social Psychology

Public Administration and Social Service Professions

Community Organization and Advocacy
Human Services, General
Public Administration
Public Administration and Social Service Professions, Other

Public Policy Analysis
Social Work
  Social Work, Other
  Youth Services/Administration

Science Technologies/Technicians

Biology Technician/Biotechnology Laboratory Technician
Nuclear and Industrial Radiologic Technologies/Technicians
  Industrial Radiologic
  Technology/Technician
  Nuclear and Industrial Radiologic Technologies/Technicians, Other

  Nuclear/Nuclear Power
  Technology/Technician
Physical Science Technologies/Technicians
  Chemical Technology/Technician
  Physical Science Technologies/Technicians, Other
Science Technologies/Technicians, Other

Security and Protective Services

Criminal Justice and Corrections
  Corrections
  Corrections Administration
  Corrections and Criminal Justice, Other
  Criminal Justice/Law Enforcement Administration
  Criminal Justice/Police Science
  Criminal Justice/Safety Studies
  Criminalistics and Criminal Science
  Forensic Science and Technology

  Juvenile Corrections
  Securities Services
  Administration/Management
  Security and Loss Prevention Services
Fire Protection
  Fire Protection and Safety Technology/Technician
  Fire Protection, Other
  Fire Science/Firefighting
  Fire Services Administration
Security and Protective Services, Other

Social Sciences

Anthropology
  Anthropology, General
  Anthropology, Other
  Physical Anthropology
Archeology
Criminology
Demography and Population Studies
Economics
  Applied Economics
  Development Economics and International Development
  Econometrics and Quantitative Economics
  Economics, General
  Economics, Other
  International Economics

Geography and Cartography
  Cartography
  Geography, General
  Geography, Other
International Relations and Affairs
Political Science and Government
  American Government and Politics (United States)
  Canadian Government and Politics
  Political Science and Government, General
  Political Science and Government, Other
Sociology
Social Sciences, General
Social Sciences, Other
Urban Studies/Affairs

Theology and Religious Vocations

Bible/Biblical Studies
Divinity/Ministry (BD, MDiv)
  Pre-Theology/Pre-Ministerial Studies
  Rabbinical Studies
  Talmudic Studies
  Theological and Ministerial Studies, Other
Missions/Missionary Studies and Missiology
Pastoral Counseling and Specialized Ministries

  Pastoral Counseling and Specialized Ministries, Other
  Pastoral Studies/Counseling
  Youth Ministry
Religious Education
Religious/Sacred Music
Theological and Ministerial Studies
Theology and Religious Vocations, Other

Transportation and Materials Moving

Air Transportation
  Aeronautics/Aviation/Aerospace Science and Technology, General
  Air Traffic Controller
  Air Transportation, Other
  Airline Flight Attendant
  Airline/Commercial/Professional Pilot and Flight Crew
  Aviation/Airway Management and Operations
  Flight Instructor
Ground Transportation

Construction/Heavy Equipment/Earth-moving Equipment Operation
  Ground Transportation, Other
  Mobil Crane Operation/Operator
  Truck and Bus Driver/Commercial Vehicle Operation
Marine Transportation
  Commercial Fishing
  Diver, Professional and Instructor
  Marine Science/Merchant Marine Officer
  Marine Transportation, Other
Transportation and Materials Moving, Other

Visual and Performing Arts

Crafts/Craft Design, Folk Art and Artisanry
Dance
  Ballet
  Dance, General
  Dance, Other
Design and Applied Arts
  Commercial and Advertising Art
  Commercial Photography
  Design and Applied Arts, Other
  Design and Visual Communications, General
  Fashion/Apparel Design
  Graphic Design
  Illustration
  Industrial Design
  Interior Design
Drama/Theatre Arts and Stagecraft
  Acting
  Directing and Theatrical Production
  Drama and Dramatics/Theatre Arts, General
  Dramatic/Theatre Arts and Stagecraft, Other
  Playwriting and Screenwriting
  Technical Theatre/Theatre Design and Technology
  Theatre Literature, History and Criticism
  Theatre/Theatre Arts Management

Film/Video and Photographic Arts
  Cinematography and Film/Video Production
  Film/Cinema Studies
  Film/Video and Photographic Arts, Other
  Photography
Fine and Studio Art
  Art History, Criticism and Conservation
  Art/Art Studies, General
  Arts Management
  Ceramic Arts and Ceramics
  Drawing
  Fiber, Textile and Weaving Arts
  Fine Arts and Art Studies, Other
  Fine/Studio Arts, General
  Intermedia/Multimedia
  Metal and Jewelry Arts
  Painting
  Printmaking
  Sculpture
Music
  Conducting
  Jazz/Jazz Studies
  Music, General
  Music History, Literature, and Theory
  Music Management and Merchandising
  Music, Other

Music Pedagogy
Music Performance, General
Music Theory and Composition
Musicology and Ethnomusicology
Piano and Organ

Violin, Viola, Guitar and Other
Stringed Instruments
Voice and Opera
Visual and Performing Arts, General
Visual and Performing Arts, Othe

Index

academic calendar (academic semester), 4, 6, 7, 100, 107
academic counseling. See counseling, school
academic English, 6
accounting profession, 81–82
accreditation (for colleges and universities), 110; what it is and why you need to know, 111; questions to ask, 113
adult education programs, 6, 8
adult students, 109, 116–117. See also adult education programs
aid, financial. See financial aid
American English, 1, 10, 12
apprenticeship, 2
assessment tests (ESL). See placement tests
associations, 35, 40, 43, 44, 45–46, 49, 51–56, 80, 88, 89
attorneys, 36, 53, 81–90
audio component (websites), 9, 10
auditing, 5, 100

bar associations, 89–90
Basic English Skills Test (BEST), 13
Better Business Bureau, 38, 154
books: academic programs at particular schools, 171; career guidance, 40–41; ESL, 10–11; Washington Metropolitan Area reference services, 155. See also counseling; courses; English courses; financial aid
British English, 1, 9
business development. See entrepreneur
business English, 7

Cambridge (exams), 12
career: books, 40–41; CIDS assessment software, 34; counselor. See counseling; guidance listings, 56–78 (for seniors, 58–59, 65–67, 74–76; by state. See District of Columbia, Maryland, suburban, and Virginia, Northern); new career paths, 37; one-stop concept, 34, 56, 62, 72; retraining, 36–37, 39–40, 43–45, 106
CDs, ESL, 2, 11
certification, 46, 101, 105
chamber of commerce, 38, 97
citizenship: and financial aid, 150; and licensure, 49; U.S. Bureau of

Citizenship and Immigration
Services (BCIS), 158
College Level Examination Program
(CLEP), 103
colleges and universities: academic
programs throughout the U.S.
(listings), 171– ; community
colleges (business, ESL courses,
2–3, 6, 14–22); credit for previous
work or prior learning (tests that
earn you credit, 102–103; transfer,
102; work experience that earns
you credit, 103); degree,
101–102; location, 114–115;
types, 6–8, 34, 109. *See also*
financial aid, institutional aid;
listings; state entries
community organizations and
agencies, 8, 34, 59, 67, 76, 145
compact discs, ESL. *See* CDs, ESL
competency-challenge exams, 103
Comprehensive Adult Student
Assessment System (CASAS), 13
Comprehensive English Language
Test (CELT), 3, 13
computer courses. *See* career,
retraining; courses, nontraditional
ways to learn and earn credit;
distance learning
consultants: *See* counseling, business
development; financial aid,
institutional aid
consumer affairs help and consumer
protection, 39, 155
continuing education departments, 4,
7, 15–22, 100
conversation groups, 8
co-op (cooperative education), 107.
See also financial aid, work-study
programs
corporate language schools. *See*
private language schools

counseling: business development,
38; career, 33, 34, 35, 36;
financial aid, 141, 147; school
(course, program), 99
course names, 2, 12, 104, 117. *See
also* programs
courses: counseling. *See* counseling,
school (course, program); ESL.
See credit for previous work. *See*
English courses; re-training;
transfer credit. *See also* career,
retraining; distance learning, 105;
noncredit, 38, 100–101;
nontraditional ways to learn and
earn credit, 99 (co-op education,
107; late-stating courses 107; off-
campus courses, 107; recreation
and sports activities, 107;
scheduling problems, ways to
help with, 99–100, 104–107;
travel-study programs, 107;
weekend courses, 107). *See also*
college, credit for previous work
credentials, 47, 49, 51; educational
institution evaluators 110–113;
foreign credential evaluators,
168–170
credit for previous work (credit for
prior learning). *See* colleges and
universities

Dantes test. *See* DSST-Dantes test
dentists, 50, 85
diplomats, 7, 8
distance learning. *See* courses,
nontraditional ways to learn and
earn credit
District of Columbia (Washington,
D.C.): career guidance (listings),
56–62; colleges and universities
(listings), 117–121; D.C.
Consumer and Regulatory Affairs

Department, 155; D.C. State
Education Office, 111; English
courses, American (listings),
14–15, 22–23, 26–27; financial
aid. *See* financial aid, state aid;
licensing boards, 80–88
doctors. *See* physicians
DSST-Dantes test, 103

education. *See* courses; career,
retraining; colleges and
universities, degree; certification
EFL (English as a foreign language).
See course names, ESL
e-mails in book, about, xi
employee, definition of, 37, 48
employment: trends, 35–36, 38, 40,
49. *See also* employee;
independent contractor; co-op;
financial aid, work-study
programs
engineering profession, 82
English courses: American (ESL,
ESOL), 2–9; 12, 14–32; levels
(academic, 6, 7, 12; advanced, 4,
7; beginning, 4, 7, 8;
intermediate, 4, 7–8; pre-
academic, 7; survival, 8); names,
2, 12; program providers
(community colleges, 4, 7, 16–22;
community organizations, 8;
continuing education departments,
4, 7, 16–22; English language
institutes, 4, 6, 15, 16, 18; ethnic
groups). *See* ethnic groups; four-
year colleges, 4, 6, 7, 13–16;
libraries, public, 8, 11; literacy
groups, 8, 21–27, 31; private
language schools, 4, 7–8, 22–26;
public school systems, adult
education courses, 4, 6, 8, 26–31;
test preparation schools, 8, 32;

universities, 4, 6, 10, 14–16);
types (intensive, 2, 4, 6, 8;
nonintensive, 2, 4, 8; online,
9–10; part-time, 8; semi-intensive,
2, 4)
English language institutes, 4, 6, 15,
16, 18
entrepreneur, 37–39, 90–97
ESL (English as a second language),
2, 9, 10. *See also* English courses
ESOL (English for/to speakers of
other languages), 2
ethnic groups, 8, 53, 94, 143

financial aid: academic common
market, 143; business funding,
38. *See also* entrepreneur;
employer assistance, 142; ESL, 6;
FAFSA, 142–143, 148, 152–153;
federal aid, 141–143, 146–152;
fellowships and internships, 142;
institutional aid (school financial
aid), 141–147, 149; loans, 141,
146, 149–151; occupation-related,
145; other aid, 146–147; private
and corporate aid, 145; SAR
(Student Aid Report), 148, 153;
scholarships, 145–147, 151; state
aid, 143, 148; work-study, 141,
149–151
first steps, 12, 40, 108, 148
four-year colleges. *See* colleges and
universities

health professions, 84–88
high technology councils, 38, 96
home-based business, 37

independent contractor, definition of,
37, 47
information technology. *See* career,
retraining

informational interview, 39. *See also*
networking
intensive English courses. *See*
English courses, types
international English, 9
international students, 6–8, 150–151
Internet resources, 2, 9–10
internships, 4–5, 142. *See also*
mentors

language lab, 6
lawyers. *See* attorneys
libraries, public (local), 8, 11–12, 38,
45, 49, 53, 62, 72, 97, 145
licensing (licensure), 36, 37, 47–51.
See also occupations
licensing board(s), 36, 47–51, 79–89
licensing exam, 50, 84–88, 90
literacy groups, 8, 26, 27–28
loans. *See* financial aid, loans

Maryland, suburban: career guidance
(listings), 62–71; colleges and
universities (listings), 121–128;
English courses, American
(listings), 15–19, 23–24, 27–29;
financial aid. *See* financial aid,
state aid; licensing boards, 81, 83,
85, 89; Maryland Higher
Education Commission, 111; State
of Maryland Consumer Protection
Hotline, 156
mentors, 38, 51. *See also*
informational interview; tutors,
ESL
Michigan Test of English Language
Proficiency, 3, 13
Microsoft. *See* certification

networking, 38, 41, 52. *See also*
informational interview

nonintensive English courses. *See*
English courses, types
Northern Virginia. *See* Virginia,
Northern
nurses, 37, 86–87, 145

occupations, licensing, 48, 80–90.
See also careers, re-training;
financial aid
online courses, ESL. See distance
learning; English courses, types

paraprofessional, 37, 44–45
part-time English courses. See
English courses, types
pharmacists, 87, 145
phone numbers in book, about using,
xi
physicians, 36, 87–88, 143
placement tests (English or ESL), 3,
5, 6, 7
portfolio program, 103–104
pre-academic courses, ESL. *See*
English courses, levels
private language schools, 4, 7–8,
22–26
pronunciation (American English), 1,
5, 10
public libraries. *See* libraries, public
public school systems, ESL courses.
See English courses, program
providers

resume, pre-resume questionnaire,
11–166

SBA (U.S. Small Business
Administration), 38
SBDC (Small Business Development
Center), 38
school financial aid. *See* financial
aid, institutional aid

semi-intensive courses, ESL. *See*
    English courses, types
Stafford loan. *See* financial aid, loans
survival English. *See* English
    courses, levels

tapes, ESL, 1, 10–11
TAST (TOEFL Academic Speaking
    Test), 3, 13
teachers, ESL, 5, 9, 10
television, English courses, 1
TESOL (teachers of English to
    speakers of other languages), 5
test preparation schools, 8–9, 31–32,
    50
tests, 3, 8, 12–13, 103. *See also*
    licensing exam
TOEFL (Test of English as a Foreign
    Language), 3, 6, 8, 13
TOEIC (Test of English for
    International Communication), 13
training. *See* career, re-training;
    courses
transfer credit. *See* colleges and
    universities, credit for prior work
TSE (Test of Spoken English), 13
tuition rates, 147
tutors, ESL, 11–12

United States agencies: Bureau of
    Citizenship and Immigration
    Services (BCIS), 158; Department

of Education, 112, 113, 149, 158;
    Department of Health and Human
    Services, 159; Department of
    Labor, 158, 159
universities, ESL courses, 3, 4, 6–7,
    14–16
USMLE (United States Medical
    Licensing Examination), 8–9, 88

Virginia, Northern: career guidance
    (listings), 72–78; colleges and
    universities (listings), 128–139;
    English courses, American
    (listings), 16, 19–22, 25–26,
    29–31; financial aid. *See* financial
    aid, state aid; licensing boards,
    81, 82–85, 89–90; State of
    Virginia Office of Consumer
    Affairs, 154
visas, student, 8, 150
vocabulary (English), technical, 4, 6,
    11

Washington, D.C. *See* District of
    Columbia
Washington metropolitan area,
    defined, ix
websites at end of chapters: audio
    component, 9–10; how to use, xi;
    listings, 9–10, 41–42, 172
work-study programs. *See* financial
    aid; co-op

ng manager at the Office of Workforce
ducation at Prince George's Community
er degree when her children were in col-
nand the need to work while attending
raditional option available to speed up the
ce costs. After receiving her B.S., she felt a
what she had learned with other adult stu-
developed a noncredit course entitled Poof!
ate, to teach students about the myriad of non-
r gaining college credit, preventing frustration,
d combining courses. Much of the course material
third chapter of this book. Maureen Ickrath also
rse to teach students how to document experiences
om, which can be evaluated for college credit. As a
, she shares her knowledge with women's groups, fra-
on, clubs, religious groups, and other organizations.

n, M.Ed. and Ed.S., has been a financial aid adminstrator
ashington University and Montogmery College. She has
recent high school graduates, returning adult learners, and
from all over the world striving to improve their lives
ucation. Ruthe Kaplan wrote the fourth chapter of this book.

owe, B.A., is a native of Lesotho, an American citizen, and a fel-
the Economic Development Institute (EDI) of the World Bank.
pent six years working with international forums of the U.N. and
World Bank, and for the last ten years has provided career informa-
to individuals and groups and maintained career center re-
rces. She has also been involved with outreach efforts to ethnic and
ulticultural communities in Montgomery County. Keke Lowe is a di-
ersity trainer for the National Multicultural Institute in Washington,
D.C. She has contributed her expertise to the second chapter of this book.

204

Maureen Ickrath is a market...
Development and Continuing ...
College. She began pursuing ...
lege, thus understands firs...
school. She used every no...
education process and red...
compelling need to shar...
dents. As a result, she ...
You're a College Grad...
traditional methods f...
staying motivated, an...
is contained in the ...
teaches a credit co...
outside the classr...
volunteer speake...
ternal organizati...

Ruthe Kapla...
at George W...
worked wit...
immigrants...
through e...

Keke L...
low at ...
She s...
the ...
tion...
so...
m...

Lesley Kamensh...
and columnist. She ...
concerns, seeking to u...
fies a path for success. S...
and Directory for Immigra...
career coach. While with th...
U.S. Small Business Developm...
shine developed and implemente...
Support Program, the first of its kin...
Through a variety of activities, her g...
clarifying a path for immigrants pursui...
though she has recently begun addressing ...
Kamenshine continuously seeks to tackle un...

Solveig Fisher has always been fascinated by lang...
the focus of her career. With a B.A. in comparative lan...
in linguistics from the University of Chicago, she begar...
cational publishing, first as a pronunciation editor for the ...
Dictionary and subsequently as associate editor of languages ...
tics for *Encyclopaedia Britannica*. Both her study of languages a...
itorial work prepared her well for teaching English as a second la...
Through the years, she has taught ESL to many different populatio...
continuing education departments, college programs, corporations, a...
factories. She is currently an associate professor in the American Engli...
language program at Montgomery College–Germantown Camp...
Solveig Fisher wrote the first chapter of this book.